纯英文版

床头灯英语·3000词读物

GREEK MYTHS
希腊神话故事

[古希腊] 佚名 / 著 · 王若平 / 主编

跟更多的人一起进步，
增值服务持续更新

北京理工大学出版社
BEIJING INSTITUTE OF TECHNOLOGY PRESS

图书在版编目（CIP）数据

希腊神话故事：英文 /（古希腊）佚名著；王若平主编．—北京：北京理工大学出版社，2019.8

ISBN 978-7-5682-7262-9

Ⅰ．①希…　Ⅱ．①佚…②王…　Ⅲ．①英语－语言读物②神话－作品集－古希腊　Ⅳ．①H319.4：I

中国版本图书馆 CIP 数据核字（2019）第 142575 号

出版发行 / 北京理工大学出版社有限责任公司
社　　址 / 北京市海淀区中关村南大街 5 号
邮　　编 / 100081
电　　话 /（010）68914775（总编室）
（010）82562903（教材售后服务热线）
（010）68948351（其他图书服务热线）
网　　址 / http://www.bitpress.com.cn
经　　销 / 全国各地新华书店
印　　刷 / 天津东辰丰彩印刷有限公司
开　　本 / 880 毫米 ×1230 毫米　1/32
印　　张 / 5.75
字　　数 / 92 千字
版　　次 / 2019 年 8 月第 1 版　2019 年 8 月第 1 次印刷
定　　价 / 12.80 元

责任编辑 / 梁铜华
文案编辑 / 梁铜华
责任校对 / 杜　枝
责任印制 / 施胜娟

图书出现印装质量问题，请拨打售后服务热线，本社负责调换

《床头灯英语丛书》
编委会

三千词读遍天下书

喜欢读有趣的故事、小说是人类的天性，世界各国的人在对文学作品进行愉快的阅读中不知不觉地掌握了自己的语言，英语学习也不例外。但很多英语学习者都有过啃不动原著的痛苦经历，没读完一行就遇到好几个生词，一页纸上密密麻麻地标注了音标和释义，坚持不了几页只得作罢。

反观汉语，我们采取了完全相反的学习模式。在 87 000 个汉字中，3 000 多个常用汉字就能覆盖现代汉语的 99%。在长达九年的义务教育中，这三四千个汉字在我们所读的大量文学作品中成千上万次再现，在超量语境的刺激下，我们对这些常用词的准确含义、搭配、用法烂熟于心，而不会为还有八万多个汉字不认识而烦恼，这使得我们的汉语得以运用自如。

同样，在英语的 100 万个词汇中，常用的 3 000 词能覆盖国外日常会话、报刊典型文章、常规工作交流所用英语的 85%，剩余 15% 并不会构成大的障碍，所以英语进阶的关键就是在大量作品的阅读中彻底掌握这 3 000 词。

本套丛书精选了西方最受欢迎的数十部文学经典，从英国女王，到比尔·盖茨、乔布斯、扎克伯格等都读过其中的作品；丛书由当代美国作家执笔，用 3 000 词以原汁原味的现代英语写成，使你躺在床上不用翻词典就可以津津有味地读下去。走进一部英文小说，你就生活在一个“英语世界”里，读几十本英文名著，相当于在美国生活两年，自然能够获得惊人的语言能力。

推 荐 序

王润霞，《床头灯英语丛书》策划者之一，资深英语教育践行者。1998 年以来她按照自己对英语教育的理解，引导女儿取得了一系列惊人的成绩：2004 年北京市高考理科第二名，托福（TOEFL）673 分（满分 677 分），清华大学电子工程系专业和综合成绩排名双项第一，获得 10 多所美国顶尖大学（普林斯顿、耶鲁、麻省理工、加州理工、斯坦福、康奈尔等）的全额奖学金，博士毕业后拿到了麦肯锡、波士顿、贝恩三大咨询公司的工作 offer。

我女儿为什么能在中国的语言环境中学好英语

我女儿是在中国语言环境中学好英语的一个代表，她的经历或许会给国内正在学或准备学英语的人一些启示，帮助他们少走弯路，最终享受到学好英语所带来的益处。当然，你可能会觉得我孩子的情况很特殊，属于个例。但是，我的英语教学体会是：**每个学生都是语言的天才，只要学习方法正确，英语没有学不好的。**这些年我一共带了几百名学生，很多考上了世界名校，如美国麻省理工学院、宾夕法尼亚大学、耶鲁大学、康奈尔大学，英国伦敦大学学院等。**这些学生都是普通的学生，关键是他们背后都站着一个大事不糊涂、肯为孩子付出、和孩子在正确道路上坚持到底的家长。**

当年我沉痛的教训，后来让孩子少走弯路

1978 年我考入哈尔滨工业大学物理师资班，从此进入教育领域，后来阴差阳错地和英语结下了不解之缘。我们那时高考是不考英语的，进入大学之前我的英语水平可以这样描述：词汇量不超过 2 位数，单词读

音都用汉字标注，能把 children 读成“秋得润”，英语课本把“工农兵”翻译成“workers, peasants, and soldiers”。上大学之后，我朦朦胧胧地感到英语比较重要，就开始认真学英语。同时把这个当时非常前卫的信息传递给了我的两个弟弟（其中一个弟弟为本书主编），并给他们买了学英语的书，先后让他们跟着广播、录音机学英语。当时中国经历了特殊历史时期，刚刚恢复高考，我们那年入学的学生年龄和背景差别都很大，有 6 个孩子的父亲，也有 3 个孩子的母亲，我们班年龄最大的 34 岁，我 17 岁。在那个年代，大家都非常珍惜这来之不易的学习机会，但学习语言年龄小还是很占优势的，我的英语轻松地取得了好成绩。转眼两年英语课结束，我们就认为英语学好了，大功告成了。

英语老师在结课时告诫大家要多读英语原版书，我就把原版书买回来，也做了计划，每天都看。第一天，看了一页，发现不认识的词比认识的词还要多，第二天也好不了多少，更要命的是看到第 10 页时已经不知道前面讲的是什么了，生词还是生词……这样坚持了 20 多天，只得放弃。其他大多数同学据说连一周都没坚持到。**多年之后我发现大部分中国人英语学不好的关键原因是所读书的难度远远超出自己的水平，台阶太陡，根本上不去，夭折了。**

转眼到了 1985 年，我大弟弟高考，英语考了 99 分（满分 100 分）。进入大学后由于他英语，尤其在语音方面，很出色，便成为学校英语广播电台的播音员。1989 年他大学毕业，以他主修的管理专业在北京找了一个多月工作都没找到。就在他绝望之际，他师兄建议他用英语这项技能尝试找工作，我说：“死马当活马医，去试试吧。”一周之内，他凭借出色的英语能力拿到了许多非常满意的工作 offer，最后选择了一家银行总行的国际部。很快，他的收入和生活条件就远远超过了和他读同一所大学、读的专业比他更辛苦、比他早毕业 7 年的我。当时我女儿 3 岁，我就下定决心将来一定让她学好英语。

有些事，不能“民主”

我小时候最喜欢去乡下大姑家玩儿，大姑父、姑姑脾气都特别好，家里非常民主，孩子们自然都很自由快乐。她们家有5个孩子，我二表姐是她家老三，上有哥姐，下有弟妹。她活泼、聪明、能干，地里的庄稼活、屋里的针线活都做得好。她是村里的孩子头儿，村里同龄的孩子大都不上学，所以她也向父母要求不上学。我姑父、姑姑对她说：“你自己可要想好了，现在不上学，将来别后悔。”她回答得斩钉截铁：“不后悔，后悔也不怪你们。”处在学龄前的我听了特别高兴，如果她不上学，我就可以随时找她去玩了。岁月飞逝，我上大学后又见过她一次，她当时境遇非常糟糕。因为不识字，眼睁睁看着好机会来了，却没有选择的权利。我怕她怨恨父母，就又重提她当年说过的话：“不后悔，后悔也不怪你们。”她哽咽着说：“我当时那么小，懂什么，现在后悔又有什么用呢！”她那种哀怨的表情让我难受了很久……

我女儿这代人本来就比较任性，在外面自由、快乐教育风气的影响下，她可不像我两个弟弟那么听话。她英语一直到初一都不好，更不喜欢学英语，有的时候还美其名曰：“我是中国人，干吗要学英语呀？”当她向我提出不学英语时，我脑海中就浮现出表姐那绝望的表情。最后我坚守了自己的原则底线：别的事可以“民主”，学英语这件事不能商量，你必须学！

专家的教诲

我在北京大学英语研究会主办、北京航空航天大学承办的《大学英语》月刊编辑部工作期间，负责每期的《英语人物访谈》专栏。在采访这些专家时，充分暴露了我这个理工女的特点，凡事刨根问底，那些专家让我受益很多……我一直铭记着原教育部大学英语指导委员会主任、复旦大学董亚芬教授就儿童英语教育说的一句话：**“如果条件不具备（没**

有合格的老师、合适的教材），就不要学，学错了比不学还可怕。”所以我一直没有让女儿去上不合格的英语培训课程，最后实在找不到合格的培训机构，就按照我对英语教育的理解，自己聘请老师办了个英语培训学校，教正确的发音、地道的英语。到女儿高考前，她大概读了类似于《床头灯英语丛书》的英语读物800多本，才有了后来的成绩。也正是有了成功的教育案例，我弟弟（王若平）和我才组织、策划了这套《床头灯英语丛书》。我们聘请了几十位美国作家对世界名著进行改编，邀请国内著名大学的教授审读，力求让中国学习者系统、有效地进行英语输入。

之所以推荐《床头灯英语丛书》，是因为它具备以下特点：

1. 语言现代、地道：由美国作家执笔，以原汁原味的现代英语写成，符合现在读者的阅读需求，使尘封的经典得以复活。

2. 通俗易懂：本套书依据科学的分级体系，用现代英语中最常用的英语单词写成，个别难词配上了简明的注解，让你躺在床上不用翻词典，就能轻松读下去。

3. 选材上乘，情节曲折：当今社会，时间成本是最昂贵的，每个想有所作为的人对于书籍的选择，尤其是外语书，必须谨慎，最好读经典。这套丛书的选材非常注意作品对读者的吸引力，比如：

《吸血鬼》（*Dracula*）：这个故事真吓人，我读完以后好几天没睡好觉。后来我的一个学生说他对英语从来不感兴趣，我就把这本小说推荐给他。后来他对我说：“这是我一口气读完的第一本英语书，就是太吓人了。老师，能不能再给我来一本？”

《呼啸山庄》（*Wuthering Heights*）：讲述的是一个骇人听闻的复仇故事，很难想象竟出自一个生活在与世隔绝环境中的女孩之手。

《飘》（*Gone with the Wind*）：很多美国女孩都读过这本书。在美国麻省理工学院，两个读博的女生在谈论如何找到合适的另一半的话题时，师姐是这样向师妹传授经验的："你去仔细把《飘》好好读读，然后你可能就有答案了。"

4. 这套读物构建了国内比较完备的英语阅读阶梯体系：包括儿童阅读、1 000 词、1 500 词、2 000 词、3 000 词、5 000 词、6 500 词等阶梯系列，每个阶梯都有很多本，读者可以根据自己的水平选择一个起点，循序渐进地展开阅读。学英语要有足够大的输入量才能形成语感。我们当年就不明白要大量阅读比较简单的读物后再上台阶的道理，结果白白错过了年轻而又充满学习热情的关键时期，导致一辈子都没办法自由地使用英语。后来在陪女儿学英语的过程中才发现：中国人学英语失败的主要原因是地道英语的输入量远远不足。而语言能力上的获得是一个长期的过程，需要大量的"输入"。没有几百万个甚至是上千万个英文单词的输入，很难掌握英语。人们总指望把某本或者某几本书读完了英语学习就能一劳永逸，殊不知，"微量阅读"是学习英语的致命方式。

5. 配有高质量的录音：这套书所配的录音是标准的美式发音，特聘教育部录音专家录制音频，音质清晰、优美，语速缓慢，非常适合英语学习者反复精听和模仿。在缺乏正确英语语音的中国语言环境下，简单、标准、地道的语音输入量严重不足，是英语学习者发音、听力、口语不好的主要原因。本套书的录音对中国英语学习者而言无疑是雪中送炭。

6. 这套书也得到了国外读者的肯定，我在美国纽约书店注意到美国读者也喜欢这套书，它是在美国少见的中国出版的图书之一。

当被问及英语学习的问题时，我经常会想起当年那些英语专家的教诲。我一直对他们心存感激，是他们的理念让我培养出一个比较优秀的女儿和一批比较出色的孩子，我也愿意把我的体会分享给那些在通向英语自由境界的路上迷茫的人。

王润霞于北京

世界著名翻译家，北京大学许渊冲教授（左）

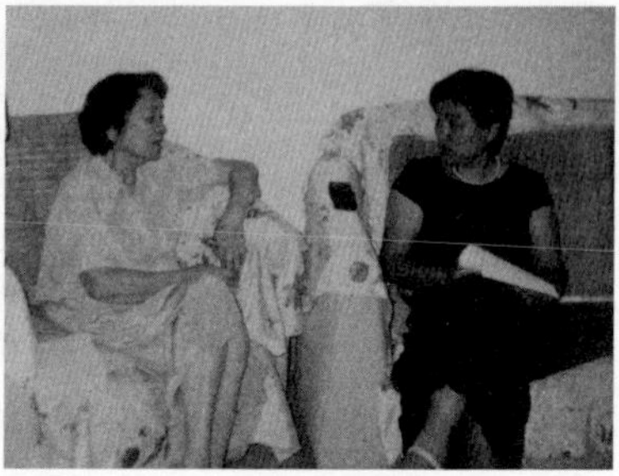

教育部第一任大学英语指导委员会主任，清华大学陆慈教授（左）

教育部第二任大学英语指导委员会主任，复旦大学董亚芬教授（国内大学英语教材鼻祖）（左）

原大学英语四六级考试委员会主任，上海交大杨惠忠教授（右）

在 MIT 参加女儿博士毕业典礼与女儿合影

名家巨擘论阅读

光学几句干巴巴的英文不行……不要总是把阅读的目的放在提高英文上，阅读首先是吸收知识，在吸收知识的过程中自然而然就吸收了语言。

——许国璋（中国英语教学的鼻祖
历任北京外国语大学英语系主任、外语研究所所长）

用英文思维是许多英语学习者都希望达到的一种境界，因为这是用英语流畅地表达思想的基础。对于一个生活在非英语环境中的中国学生来说，要做到部分或全部用英文来思考的确有很大难度，但也不是可望而不可即。从自己学习英语的经历中，我体会到坚持大量阅读是实现这一目标最有效的途径之一。

——何其莘（北京外国语大学副校长、博士生导师）

对于初、中级英语学习者我特别推荐英语简易读物，读的材料要浅易，故事性要强，读的速度尽可能快一些，读得越多越好。这是学英语屡试不爽的好方法。

——胡文仲（北京外国语大学教授）

要学好英语，就要对语言本身及语言所传达的各种文化信息感兴趣。当你读到或听到别人用简洁的英语表达深奥的思想时，兴奋不已，立即记住，这就表明你已对语言产生了兴趣。没有这种兴趣，难以在语言学习中登堂入室。

简易读物对打好基础极有用，要多读。一是数量要多，至少读 40 本。

二是要重复读，选出 10 ~ 15 本，读 3 遍。

——梅仁毅（北京外国语大学副校长、博士生导师、美国研究中心主任）

美国脱口秀大王奥普拉·温弗瑞是最富有、最有影响力的美国女人之一，她把读书称作“my personal path to freedom”（我的自由之路），她那句“The most successful people all tend to have one thing in common: They read”激荡了美国年轻的一代。

微软创始人比尔·盖茨说：“人和人的生命曲线很不同，突破人生局限的最好办法是读书。”他年轻的时候读了许多科幻小说，现在保持每年读 50 本书的习惯，《了不起的盖茨比》他和妻子读了无数遍。

特斯拉总裁马斯克是个对知识充满渴望的读者。小时候在南非经常受欺负，是科幻小说赋予他灵感和动力，使他创造出新的硅谷传奇。当被问到如何学习建造火箭时，他回答说：“I read books.”

沃伦·巴菲特在被问到成功的经验时，他指着一摞书说：“每天读 500 页，那就是知识起作用的方式，它像复利一样地积累。你们所有人都做得到，但我保证你们中没有多少人会去做。”

脸书创始人扎克伯格 17 岁前很喜欢读科幻小说，现在每两周读一本书，是读书使他保持了永久的创造力，他最喜欢这句：“All children are artists. The problem is how to remain an artist once you grow up.”

推 荐 语

1. 这套《床头灯英语丛书》，囊括了诸多英语名著，都是我们这代人在青少年时期曾汲取营养、启迪审美、塑造三观的世界文学经典之作，或思想蕴涵深厚，或行文清新细腻，或情节曲折感人，都有很高的文学审美价值和语言学习价值。

要让青少年真正地爱读名著，社会、老师和家长要形成一种合力，从高处着眼，从细处入手，激发阅读兴趣，引导阅读方式，营造阅读氛围，做好高质量的阅读陪伴。《床头灯英语丛书》是阅读经典与实用学习的得兼之作，值得青少年朋友们阅读学习。

——师传宝

中国外语教育研究中心中小学英语教育研究中心秘书长、

英语周报社副总编辑

2. 想学好英语，多读经典好书是捷径之一。《床头灯英语丛书》有语言、有思维、有文化、有审美、有情感、有人生百味。英语名谚说："Reading is to the mind what exercise is to the body." 运动强健躯体，阅读滋养灵魂。快来把阅读变成你的生存方式吧！它将给你一双隐形的翅膀，让你的人生从此自由而丰满。

——陈力

人民教育出版社编审、《义务教育课程标准实验教科书英语(新版)》责编

3. 阅读给我们打开了一扇窗。透过窗我们看到了别人，也看到了世界，通过这扇窗，我们也更好地看到了自己。

——陈新忠

北京教育科学研究院基础教研中心英语教研员、

教育部《高中课程标准》修订组核心成员

4. 我有一位同事，他是数学教师，但英语学得很棒。我曾经问他："你的英语学得如此地道纯正，有什么秘诀吗？"他坦诚回答："我只是读了几本床头灯英语小说。"可见，对于学习英语而言，名著阅读可以起到事半功倍的作用，也完全符合英语课程标准的理念。

——何书利

北京教育学院朝阳分院教师专业发展中心主任、

北京市英语学科骨干教师

5. 20 世纪 60 年代，我也是中学生，曾经阅读过所推荐书目中的大部分简写本，夯实了基础，开阔了思维，增加了兴趣，让我受益良多。我号召中学生朋友们翻开书，一本本读，会大有裨益！

——范存智

北大附中资深英语教师、人民教育出版社新课标教材培训教师、

北京教育考试院高考和会考试卷评价课题组成员、英语沙龙杂志顾问、

北京教育出版社教育科学研究院副院长

导　读

西方文明在整个人类文明中占有重要的地位。西方文明的核心是由“两希”构成。一个是希伯来文化，其最高成就为犹太人创作的《圣经》，它是西方文明发源的灵感源泉之一；另一个是比希伯来文化更为古老的希腊文化，其辉煌灿烂文化的种子就包孕在希腊神话史诗中。

作为西方文化的根源，希腊神话对世界的影响无疑是巨大的。本书波澜壮阔的文化氛围、悲壮的历史、光怪陆离的故事，为读者掀开了那令世界难以忘怀的扉页，敞开了一扇观察和认识古希腊乃至欧洲文化的窗口。内容包括潘多拉魔盒、俄耳甫斯与欧律狄刻的生死恋、九头蛇怪海德拉、亚马逊女战士、金苹果、雅典娜女神、泰坦擎天神、迈达斯国王的点金术、金羊毛……

希腊神话的核心是以人为本，歌颂了人的美好，坚信人的力量，虽名为神话，实为人的神话。

Contents

Pandora's Box

When the gods created the earth, they made it a perfect place for man. Each of the gods gave man a gift, such as strength, intelligence, and skills, and they filled the earth with everything that man needed to live happily. Fruit trees grew everywhere, and beautiful flowers gave out a delicious drink called nectar① that gave people energy. No people needed to work or hunt, and people never grew old or sick or died.

The only thing that the gods did not give man was fire. This they kept for themselves. They feared that giving man fire would make him as powerful as the gods and would cause him to destroy the many wonderful things that the gods had put on Earth.

One day, the Titan② named Prometheus③ stole some fire from heaven and gave it to man.

① **nectar** /'nektə/ *n.* 神酒，任何美味的饮料，花蜜，甘露

② **Titan**【希神】泰坦，太阳神，巨人。

③ **Prometheus**【希神】普罗米修斯（造福于人类的神），传说普罗米修斯是从奥林匹斯偷火给人类的巨人，因为这事宙斯（Zeus）将他锁在一块巨石上，派一只鹰去吃他的肝，而他的肝每天又重新长上。

Though man knew that fire was the possession of the gods, they still accepted Prometheus' gift. Zeus① was very angry at this and decided to punish man. He called on Hephaestus②, the god of metal and fire, and asked him to build a woman out of stone. Aphrodite③, the goddess of love, modeled for the statue so that it would be beautiful. When it was finished, Athena④ breathed life into the cold stone and it came alive. Then each of the gods gave the woman a gift. Aphrodite taught her how to dance and how to attract any man without even having to look at him. Athena gave her great wisdom. Apollo⑤ taught her how to play many musical instruments, and the Muse's⑥ taught her how to sing. Hermes taught her how to tell wonderful lies that made other people happy. The last gift was given to her by Hera⑦, Zeus' wife, and this was curiosity. The gods then named her Pandora, which

① **Zeus**【希神】宙斯，希腊神话中的主神，天堂的统治者，其他神和人间英雄的父亲（赫拉的丈夫）。

② **Hephaestus**【希神】赫菲斯托斯，火和锻冶之神。

③ **Aphrodite**【希神】阿佛洛狄忒，爱与美的女神。

④ **Athena**【希神】雅典娜，智慧与技艺的女神。

⑤ **Apollo**【希神】阿波罗，司预言、音乐、医药、诗歌之神，美男子、太阳神。

⑥ **Muse**【希神】掌管文艺、美术、音乐等的缪斯女神。

⑦ **Hera**【希神】赫拉，主神宙斯的妻子，司妇女与婚嫁的女神。

means "All-gifted" and placed her down on Earth with all the common men.

Zeus went down to Earth with Pandora and gave her one last gift. It was a beautiful box, closed with a heavy lock. He then gave Pandora the key to the box and told her that she must never open it, or let anybody else open it for any reason.

After a short time, one of Prometheus' brothers, Epimetheus[①], met Pandora and fell deeply in love with her. She loved him as well and returned with him to his small village. They lived there together happily because life was easy and there were no troubles. The people of the village spent their days dancing and singing in the warm sunshine. Plenty of food grew on the trees and clean water ran through the rivers. Also, since nobody ever grew old or became ill, there was no way to die or lose a friend, family member, or a lover. Everyone's life on Earth was perfect.

Though Pandora was happy living with Epimetheus, she could not forget the box that Zeus had given her. This was because Hera had given her the

① **Epimetheus**【希神】埃庇米修斯，普罗米修斯的兄弟。

gift of curiosity, and each day Pandora's curiosity grew bigger and bigger inside her. But she followed Zeus' order and put the box in a corner of their home where she would not have to look at it. She then told Epimetheus not to ever touch it or move it.

One night, after a few years in the village, Pandora woke up in the middle of the night and walked into the room where the box was. The moonlight was shining in through the window, and it made the box look bright and wonderful. The box itself was not fancy[①] or special. It was just a common box with a large lock on the front. Pandora reached into her pocket and felt the key inside for she had kept the key there since Zeus had given it to her. The key felt warm in her hand and sent excitement through her body. Her curiosity grew and grew as she walked closer and closer to the box, but then she remembered Zeus' words and turned away.

She got back into bed with Epimetheus, but was not able to sleep. She kept thinking about the box and wondering what was inside. Finally, Pandora got up and went to the room where the box sat.

① **fancy** /ˈfænsɪ/ *adj.* 精致的；绚丽的

She carried the box outside into the garden, dug a deep hole in the middle of a group of flowers, and placed the box inside. She looked down at it one last time before covering it with the earth. She then took several large stones and piled them on top of the hole. She was tired from her work and returned to bed to sleep with Epimetheus.

As she slept, she had a dream about the box. In her dream, the box was bright and beautiful, and it softly whispered① her name over and over again, "Pandora... Pandora..." it said. Then she took the key out of her pocket and carefully inserted it into the lock. As she turned the key, the box became even brighter and more beautiful. When she opened the top, she was amazed because the box was filled with the most beautiful jewels that she had ever seen! These were her gift from Zeus! But why wasn't she supposed to open it? With those jewels, she and Epimetheus could live like a King and Queen!

She awoke from her dream and sat up in bed. It was still dark, and Epimetheus was asleep at

① **whisper** /ˈwɪspə/ *vt.* 低声说；私语

her side. She jumped out of bed and ran out to her garden. Her hands quickly pushed away the rocks that sat over the hole. She moved the heavy rocks so quickly that her hands began to bleed, but she didn't notice because there was not yet pain or suffering in the world. She dug into the earth and didn't stop until she felt the top of the box. Grasping the box with excitement, she pulled it out of the hole and placed it on the earth beside her. Almost without realizing it, she put her hand into her pocket and pulled out the key.

For a short moment, Pandora looked at the key lying in her hand. The metal was cold, and Pandora had never felt cold before. Unable to stop what she had begun, Pandora put the key into the lock. The feeling of cold ran through her body quickly, but she ignored[①] it. She opened the lock and threw the top of the box open.

Suddenly a thick, black smoke poured out of the box and came into her eyes. She felt something that she had never felt before: it was pain. She could not see clearly and began to cry. When her

① **ignore** /ɪgˈnɔː/ *vt.* 忽视；对……装作不知

vision[①] returned, she looked down to see thousands of tiny monsters[②] escaping from the box. They were running and flying out of the box in all directions, spreading out into the world. She grabbed one of the monsters in her hand, and it bit one of her fingers. She immediately became ill from the bite, and her body fell down onto the box causing its top to close. She lay on the ground with the box in her arms breathing heavily and feeling the sickness that the monster had given her filled her body.

After a minute, she heard a small voice cry out, "Please open the lid of the box."

Pandora listened to the voice and worried that it was just another little monster trying to trick her. "Why should I let you out," she cried, "I've already caused so much damage!"

"Please let me out of the box," said the voice. "I'm not like the others. I can help to fix what you have done. I can reduce the pain and suffering of mankind." With her last bit of strength, Pandora opened the top and then fell back down onto the

① **vision** /ˈvɪʒən/ *n.* 视力；视觉

② **monster** /ˈmɒnstə/ *n.* 怪物

earth. A small, golden light then appeared before her. When Pandora looked at it, she saw that it was a small woman with a pair of wings. The tiny woman came down to Pandora's face and kissed her lightly on the nose. Suddenly, Pandora's suffering lessened[①], and she had the strength to sit up again.

The tiny woman hung in the air before her face, "I am called Hope," she said. "I am the last of the things in the box. Through your curiosity, you have released[②] many terrible forces into the world. Each of these forces has a name: Old Age, Sickness, Misery, Selfishness, Greed, and Ugliness. The people of earth will no longer live easy lives, but I am the Hope that will give them the strength to fight these forces. I wish that I could do more, but that is the best that can be done."

Then Hope flew away and a golden light followed her. From that day on, people began to get sick, grow old, and die. But they would always have Hope to help them. This was the punishment[③] of Zeus upon men for taking fire from the gods.

---

① **lessen** /'lesən/ *vi.* 减轻；减少

② **release** /rɪ'li:s/ *vt.* 释放；解除

③ **punishment** /'pʌnɪʃmənt/ *n.* 刑罚，惩罚

Orpheus[①] and Eurydice

Orpheus was not just any ordinary man. He was the son of the god Apollo and the Muse of music, Calliope[②]. His father gave him a magical lyre[③] when he was just a young boy and taught him to play sweet music upon it. By the time he was a young man, he played his instrument so perfectly that the heart of every man, woman, and child filled with warmth when they heard him. Even the animals and plants listened to him. When the wild animals heard his music, they gathered around him in a circle; when the trees listened, their leaves grew faster; the flowers turned their heads toward the sound; even the hard rock became softer when Orpheus played.

The gods themselves loved Orpheus' playing and sent a beautiful woman called Eurydice[④] to him to be his wife. Orpheus loved Eurydice more

① **Orpheus**【希神】俄耳甫斯，歌手，善弹竖琴。

② **Calliope**【希神】卡利俄珀，司辩论、史诗的女神。

③ **lyre** /ˈlaɪə/ *n.* 七弦琴；小竖琴

④ **Eurydice**【希神】欧律狄刻，歌手俄耳甫斯之妻。

than anything in the world, more than riches, more than music, more than himself. But Orpheus and Eurydice's marriage was not a lucky one. Not long after their marriage, Eurydice was wandering in the fields, singing, and dancing, when she was seen by a lonely man called Aristaeus①. Aristaeus was amazed with Eurydice's beauty and was determined to have her. He followed her through the fields with the hope of catching her. When Eurydice saw him, she was filled with fear and ran away as fast as she could. Because she was not watching where she was going, she stepped on a snake in the grass. The snake bit her, and she died.

When Orpheus found her body, he begged the gods to let her live, but his cries were not heard. For days he cried beside her body, not eating or sleeping. Finally, Orpheus decided to go down into Hades② "the land of the dead" and find his wife. He asked Apollo, his father, to tell him where the entrance to Hades was, and Apollo led him to a cave on the side of a great cliff. Smoke poured out of the mouth of the cave and terrible screams could be heard from

① **Aristaeus**【希神】阿里斯泰俄斯。

② **Hades**【希神】冥王哈得斯 **hades** /ˈheɪdiːz/ *n.*【口】地狱；冥府。

inside, but Orpheus' love for Eurydice, and his determination to find her, were so great that he was not afraid.

He entered into the cave and instantly the light of the world outside disappeared. Great crowds of ghosts[①] surrounded him as he walked down the long staircase[②] into the center of Hades. They whispered terrible words that Orpheus could not understand. A normal man would have been killed quickly on entering Hades, but Orpheus had his lyre and played such sweet music that the guards of the underworld let him pass.

After many hours the stairs finally ended and Orpheus arrived in the center of Hades. The god of Hades sat in his great chair with his wife, and Orpheus bowed before them. Orpheus then began to play his lyre and sing:

"Great gods of the underworld,
to whom all men must one day come,
please hear my words,
for they are true and from my deepest heart.

① **ghost** /gəʊst/ *n.* 鬼怪；鬼魂

② **staircase** /ˈsteəkeɪs/ *n.* 楼梯；楼梯间

I have not come to spy on[①] your secrets,
or to test my strength against the monsters of this world.
I have come to find my wife,
who was taken from me too early by the bite of a snake.
I have come here for love.
Love, the most powerful of the gods of the men
who live on the earth, and, I believe,
a powerful god here as well.
I beg you, great gods who have the greatest power,
please return my wife to me and let her live again.
All men will come to you in time,
and Orpheus and Eurydice will both return to serve you.
But let her live again,
just for the time of a common life on Earth,
so that she can stand by my side.
If you will not do this,
I cannot return alone;

① **spy on** 侦查；暗中监视

I will stay here in the underworld."

As he sang these words and played his lyre, all the ghosts of Hades cried great tears. Then for the first time, it is said, the king of Hades himself let a single tear fall from his eye. Orpheus moved quickly and caught the tear and held it in his hand. The god then said, "You have moved my heart, Orpheus, and I will give you what you ask. You may take your wife out of Hades on one condition: You must walk up the stairs out of Hades and not turn back to look at her or this world. Not until you have arrived back in the world of the living can you turn around. If you wish to see your wife, just look into my tear that you now hold in your hand and you will see her, like in a mirror, behind you."

Orpheus began the long walk up the stairs, all the while holding the god's single tear up in front of him to see his wife behind him. In the tear he saw Eurydice following behind him as best she could. Her foot still hurt from the snake bite, and she walked slowly and silently. The stairs were dark and high, and Eurydice often slipped because of her hurt foot. Each time she slipped, Orpheus wished to run to her, but knew he could not. They walked an hour, and a terrible thought appeared in Orpheus' head. "What if Hades has tricked me into leaving the land of the dead, and Eurydice is not really behind me?"

This thought became bigger and bigger inside of Orpheus' head, until he could not think of anything else. He called out to Eurydice, begging her to answer him, but heard no reply. In truth, Eurydice was calling to him loudly, but the dead made no sound to the living. Finally Orpheus could not bear it any longer and took a quick look behind him. The moment he did this, many servants of Hades flew down and grasped Eurydice. As they pulled her back into Hades, Orpheus ran up to her and grasped her hand. They touched each other one last time before she was pulled away.

Eurydice looked at her husband with deep love and did not blame him for his impatience. How could she be angry at his desire to see her? "Goodbye, my love," she said, "a final goodbye." She then disappeared into the darkness.

Suddenly Orpheus found himself back in the light

of the world. The entrance to the cave was covered with large rocks that he could not move. He begged the gods to let him back into Hades to try one more time, but he received no answer. He sat at the cave entrance for three days and nights, without food or water. He then played his lyre and sang a song so sad that everything that heard it felt that their heart would break. The wild animals could not bear to hear a song so sad and begged him to stop. Orpheus refused, and the animals, crazy with sadness, attacked① him and pulled him into hundreds of tiny pieces.

His spirit, free from his body, fell happily into Hades where he sought out② his Eurydice and held her in his arms. They still walk together happily in Hades, with him playing the lyre and her singing, and Orpheus may look at her as much as he wishes, without fear of her disappearing from his arms.

① **attack** /ə'tæk/ *vt.* 攻击，进攻

② **seek out** 寻找到；找出

The Labors of Hercules

The Son of Zeus—Hercules

Princess Alcmene① was so beautiful and kind that every man who saw her fell immediately in love with her. Even Zeus, king of all the gods, looked down at Alcmene from his throne in the sky and fell deeply in love with her beauty. Zeus wished to take her as his bride, so he visited her one night and they were secretly married. Later Alcmene gave birth to② a son and named him Hercules③. Since Hercules was the son of Zeus, his strength was greater than any other man's.

Hera was Zeus's wife in Olympus④ the land of the gods. She knew how much her husband liked beautiful women, and was jealous of Princess Alcmene. Hera wanted greatly to see her die, but

① **Alcmene**【希神】阿尔克墨涅，底比斯（Thebes）国王安菲特律翁（Amphitryon）之妻，与宙斯通奸后生下 Hercules（赫拉克勒斯）。

② **give birth to** 生（孩子），生育

③ **Hercules**【希神】赫拉克勒斯，阿尔克墨涅（Alcmene）与宙斯（Zeus）通奸所生之子，是位力大无比的英雄，因完成宙斯之妻赫拉（Hera）要求的十二项任务而获得永生。

④ **Olympus** /əʊˈlɪmpəs/ 奥林匹斯山，天堂

Zeus ordered her not to hurt Alcmene, and Hera feared Zeus' anger. Instead Hera decided to get her revenge① on Alcmene through her son, Hercules. When Hercules was just a baby, Hera sent two huge snakes into his nursery. Hercules wrestled② with the two snakes and killed them. Even as a baby, his strength was great.

During his life, Hera did many things to try and hurt Hercules. After Hercules was married and had two children, Hera decided it was a good time to take her revenge. She made Hercules think that his wife had been sleeping with another man and that his children were not his own. Hercules became so crazy with anger that he broke his wife's neck and threw his children into a fire. When he realized the terrible deed③ that he had done, he was so filled with sadness that he left his city and lived alone in a small cave in the mountains.

For many months, Hercules stayed in the mountain cave and did not leave to see anyone. He thought about what he had done and prayed to the

① **revenge** /rɪˈvendʒ/ *n.* 报复，复仇

② **wrestle** /ˈresl/ *vi.* 搏斗

③ **deed** /diːd/ *n.* 行为；行动

gods to end his terrible sadness. The gods met together to decide what to do with Hercules. They were angry about his violent act, but they also felt that he had done some great things in his life and should receive a second chance. The gods finally decided that Hercules would be forgiven if he used his strength for good①.

Apollo, the messenger② of the gods, flew to Hercules' cave and delivered this message:

"Powerful Hercules, you must travel to Argos③ and complete twelve tasks for your cousin Eurystheus. Once you have completed these tasks, the gods will forgive you and your sadness can end." Hercules bowed to Apollo and thanked the gods for their wisdom and for giving him a second opportunity. He then left for Argos to see his cousin Eurystheus.

---

① **good** /gʊd/ *n.* 善行

② **messenger** /ˈmesɪndʒə/ *n.* 送信者，使者

③ **Argos** 阿尔戈斯，古希腊的一个城邦，位于伯罗奔尼撒半岛东北部，靠近阿尔戈利斯湾上方。青铜器时代早期开始有人居住，在斯巴达兴盛前是古希腊最强盛的城邦之一。

The Lion of Nemea

Eurystheus had always hated Hercules. He was a weak king, and was very jealous of Hercules' strength, courage, and fame, even though the two were cousins. When Hercules met with him and explained the gods' order, King Eurystheus gave Hercules an evil smile. He was very pleased.

"You are my slave now, Hercules," began the king, "and you may not leave here until you have completed all twelve tasks that I assign[①] you."

Because of his hatred[②] for Hercules, Eurystheus decided that he would find tasks that were impossible to complete. In this way, Hercules would have to spend his whole life as Eurystheus' slave. With this in his mind, the king gave his first order:

"I have decided on my first task. In the forest of Nemea[③] lives a terrible lion, which has been

① **assign** /əˈsaɪn/ *vt.* 布置，分配，给予

② **hatred** /ˈheɪtrɪd/ *n.* 仇恨，憎恶

③ **Nemea** 尼米亚，古希腊阿戈利斯北部的山谷。那里的宙斯神殿是公元前573年后尼米亚运动会的所在地。

attacking people in the towns nearby. The lion has magical skin that no weapon can break. I want you to kill this lion and bring me his skin."

Hercules traveled to the forest of Nemea in search of the troublesome[①] lion. He eventually found the animal sleeping in its cave and walked up quietly so that the lion would not hear him. Pulling out his sword, Hercules struck[②] the lion with all of his great strength. His sword broke into a hundred small pieces when it hit the lion's magic skin.

The lion awoke when he felt the attack and jumped at Hercules. Still, Hercules was the stronger of the two and used his great hands to crush[③] the lion's neck. The lion could not breathe and it fell down dead on the ground.

Hercules still faced another problem though: He needed to get the lion's skin off of its body. "But how?" he wondered. His knife would not go through the skin. Then Hercules had an idea. He grasped one of the lion's hands and tried using its own claws to cut through the magic skin. Using this method,

① **troublesome** /ˈtrʌblsəm/ *adj.* 令人讨厌的；令人烦恼的

② **strike** /straɪk/ *vt.* 打；击

③ **crush** /krʌʃ/ *vt.* 挤；榨；压碎

the lion's skin came off easily.

Hercules had another idea as well. Since the lion's skin could not be hurt by swords or arrows, he would make it into a coat of armor[①] to protect him on other adventures. He cut the skin into a coat and made the lion's head into a hat. Then he returned to see Eurystheus.

When he arrived at the king's castle, he was still wearing the lion's skin. The king was not a brave man; when he saw Hercules wearing the lion's skin, he thought that it was a lion walking on two legs. The king screamed, ran into his bedroom, and shut the door. Hercules laughed hard at the king, as did the king's guards who saw the whole scene.

① **armor** /ˈɑːmə/ *n.* 铁甲，盔甲

The Horrible Hydra

Eurystheus was embarrassed[①] and angry when he heard everyone laughing at him. Still, he was so scared that he would not leave his room and see Hercules in the lion's skin. He ordered one of his servants to tell Hercules of his second task.

"In the lake of Lerna," began the servant, "lives a terrible monster[②] called the Hydra.[③] The Hydra is a large dragon with nine heads, and the head in the middle cannot be wounded. At night, the dragon comes out of the water and eats people in the towns near the lake. The king wants you to save these towns from the Hydra."

Hercules knew that this would be a very hard task indeed, so he called for the help of his nephew Iolaus. "I must go on a very dangerous journey, Iolaus, and I will need your help," he said. Iolaus agreed, and the two men set out to find the Hydra.

---

① **embarrassed** /ɪmˈbærəst/ *adj.* 困窘的；尴尬的

② **monster** /ˈmɔnstə/ *n.* 一个想象或传说中的由各种兽形或人形组成的怪物，如半人半马；外表奇特或恐怖的动物。

③ **Hydra**【希神】海德拉，九头蛇怪，赫拉克勒斯所杀死的一个多头怪物。

When they arrived in the town nearest to the lake where the Hydra lived, Hercules asked the people about the terrible monster. He learned that many men had come to fight the Hydra, but that all had been eaten. The Hydra's strength was found in its terrible heads. If a man was able to cut off one of the monster's heads, it would instantly grow back. And no man could hurt the middle head in any way.

"This is a terrible monster indeed!" thought Hercules. "I cannot use my sword to destroy it, for its heads cannot be killed."

But Hercules was a smart man and wise[①] in the ways of fighting. He had beaten the terrible Lion of Nemea, and he felt sure he could destroy the Hydra. He asked the people of the town to make him a large net with large stones tied around the outside ropes. He then asked Iolaus to make a few torches[②] that would burn with hot flame. Once all these preparations were made, Hercules and Iolaus left to find the Hydra.

① **wise** /waɪz/ *adj.* 聪明的，有智慧的

② **torch** /tɔːtʃ/ *n.* 火把

Hercules knew that the Hydra only came out of the water at night, so he and Iolaus waited by the lake until the sun began to go down behind the hills. Hercules then told Iolaus to light the torches while he prepared the net. "Iolaus," he said, "when I cut off one of the Hydra's heads, you must quickly burn the neck so that a new head cannot grow in its place."

Just then, the two men heard the water moving. Nine huge snake heads rose out of the water. When the Hydra saw Hercules, it attacked him with all of its mouths at once. Hercules jumped back and threw the net over the monster. Because the net had heavy rocks tied around it, the monster could not move. However, this did not stop the monster from attacking. Its heads were narrow enough to get through the net and each one worked to free itself.

Each time a head became free, Hercules would cut it off with a powerful strike with his sword, and Iolaus would burn the neck with his torch. In that way, no new heads could grow where the old ones had been cut off.

Soon only the Hydra's middle head remained[①]. It rushed at Iolaus and bit his arm. Hercules jumped to help his nephew and wrestled the head down to the ground. Once the head was in his strong grasp, Iolaus tied the mouth closed with a rope.

Since the middle head was immortal[②], there was no way to kill it. Because of this, Hercules lifted the Hydra above his head and carried it up the side of the closest mountain. Once he found a cave, Hercules put the Hydra inside and closed off the entrance to the cave with many large stones. Even today, the Hydra still lives in that cave.

① **remain** /rɪˈmeɪn/ *vi.* 剩余，剩下

② **immortal** /ɪˈmɔːtəl/ *adj.* 不朽的；永世的；不死的

The Wild Pig

Hercules' third task was to find a special deer with golden horns. This deer ran so fast that no hunter had ever been able to catch it, but Hercules found it and killed it easily with his bow.

After completing this task, King Eurystheus ordered Hercules to catch a famous wild pig that had been hurting some of the farmers in a nearby town. The king felt that this task was too easy for Hercules, and Eurystheus still secretly hoped that Hercules would fail in one of his tasks so that he would have to be his slave forever. To make the task harder, King Eurystheus asked Hercules to bring the wild pig back to him alive.

As he walked to the town where the wild pig lived, Hercules thought about the king's request. He knew that his cousin was jealous of him, and wanted him to fail at one of the tasks. However, Hercules knew he wouldn't fail in a task as easy as this one! "I have killed many animals easily!" he thought.

When he arrived at the town, he asked for two cooking pots and some rope. After he obtained[①] these items, he began walking up the mountain while hitting the two pots together. "Clang[②]! Clang! Clang! Clang! Clang!" went the pots.

When the wild pig heard the sound it became so scared that it ran up the mountain. Hercules followed the pig, still hitting the pots together. Eventually the wild pig was scared into running to the very top of the mountain. Once the wild pig had no more place to run, Hercules grasped it tightly and tied it up with the rope.

The people of the town were so happy to see the wild pig tied up that they had a great party to thank Hercules. "Let's kill the wild pig and eat him!" suggested one of the villagers, but Hercules shook his head.

"I have other plans for this pig." he said.

When Hercules arrived back at the castle, Eurystheus was still in his bedroom. Hercules took the ropes off the pig and let it free in the great hall. He then went to see his cousin and told him that he

① **obtain** /əbˈteɪn/ *vt.* 获得，得到
② **clang** /klæŋ/ *n.* 叮当声；铿锵声

had brought the pig back. Now, King Eurystheus thought that the pig would certainly be tied up and walked into his great hall to see the animal. Just imagine his surprise to find the pig running around wild! The king jumped onto a table out of fear and, again, Hercules laughed at the weak king.

Cleaning the Stables

Of course, King Eurystheus was very angry at Hercules, because he had once again been embarrassed in front of his men. Because of this, Eurystheus thought of the dirtiest and most awful job he could. "Hercules," said the king, "King Augeas[①] has ten thousand cows which he cares for very much. The king keeps his cows in stables[②] near his castle. Of course, the stables are very large. Because of their size, no one has been able to clean them in many years. Your next task is to clean them so that they look like new."

Hercules thought that this was a very awful task indeed, but he did not want to let his cousin see that he was upset. Therefore he put a smile on his face and said, "Why[③], Cousin, this is an easy task. I will return to you in a few days!"

① **Augeas**【希神】王国名，取 Augean 的寓意（极肮脏的，极污秽的）。

② **stable** /ˈsteɪbəl/ *n.* 马厩，马房

③ **why** /waɪ/ *int.*（表示惊奇、怀疑、异议、承认、发现、停顿、思考等的）感叹词
Why, it's nearly nine o'clock. 啊，快要九点了。
Why, even a child knows that! 哎呀，这连小孩都知道！

When Hercules arrived in the land of King Augeas, he first went to introduce himself. "I am Hercules. My cousin has sent me here to clean your great stables."

"I know who you are, Hercules, for your fame is known everywhere. You are welcome to stay in my land as long as you want," the king said.

The next day, Hercules went out to the stables to think of how to clean them. Truly, they were so dirty that they could not be cleaned by one man, or even many hundred. He noticed that the stables were at the bottom of a large hill and that a river ran along the top of the hill. This gave him an idea.

The next day he went to see King Augeas and told him, "Great king, I can clean your stables for you in just one day, but you must first take all of your cows out into the fields."

Of course, Augeas did not believe that Hercules could complete his task in just one day, but he wanted his stables cleaned so much that he ordered his men to take all of the cows out into the fields. When this was done, Hercules climbed up the hill above the stables and found a sharp[①] rock. He used this rock to dig a hole leading from the river into the stables. As the river water flowed through the stables, all the dirt inside was cleaned away. When the stables were clean, Hercules again filled the hole with dirt and allowed the river to continue with its natural flow.

Hercules then returned to see his cousin. When he arrived, King Eurystheus could not believe that Hercules had completed his task so quickly. Only three days had passed since Hercules had left him! But later that day, a messenger arrived from King Augeas thanking Hercules for his great deed. When he heard the news, King Eurystheus was very angry.

① **sharp** /ʃɑːp/ *adj.* 敏锐的；锋利的

The Amazons

Hercules' next task was done for Eurystheus' daughter, Admete. "There is something I want, Hercules," she began. "On the north side of the Black Sea lives a group of fighting women called the Amazons①. They have no husbands and no men live within their society. Their queen is called Hippolyte②, and she wears a beautiful dress covered with jewels. I want that dress!"

Hercules knew that this task could be very dangerous and that he could not handle all of the Amazons by himself. Because of this, Hercules gathered together a group of strong fighters and they left to face the Amazons together. They traveled many months to find the land where the Amazons lived and saw many strange lands and strange people along the way.

When they arrived at the castle of Queen Hippolyte, Hercules expected a terrible fight. To his

① **Amazon**【希神】亚马逊，相传是曾居住在黑海边的女战士族，她们都是魁梧而有男子气概的妇女，彪悍强壮的妇女，高大的、咄咄逼人的、意志坚强的妇女。

② **Hippolyte**【希神】亚马逊“女儿国”女王希波吕忒。

surprise, the queen welcomed him with kindness. She had never seen a man so strong and handsome as Hercules and said, "Please come in. I will have a great meal prepared for you and your men."

While they ate Hippolyte asked Hercules why he had come to the land of the Amazons. Hercules was a brave and honest man and answered her truthfully:

"Great queen, my men and I do not wish any harm on you and your people, but I have come to ask for that dress you wear."

Hercules then explained about the tasks he had to complete to satisfy the gods and free himself from his service to his cousin. The queen listened, and was not angry. "You may have my dress," Hippolyte said, looking at Hercules with hungry eyes,"but not until tomorrow. Tonight, I wish for you to sleep in my bedroom with me. Tomorrow you can leave with what you have come for."

Hercules' task was not going to be easy. All this time, the goddess Hera had been watching Hercules, and looking for ways to keep him from succeeding in his tasks. That night, while Hercules slept with

Hippolyte, Hera transformed[1] herself into an Amazon and walked among the other women, telling them that Hercules had come to steal their queen away from them. When they heard this, the Amazons attacked Hercules and his men.

A great battle began and Hercules and his men were forced to kill many Amazons. Hercules felt terrible about killing women and was especially unhappy when he had to face Hippolyte in a fight. She was a fierce fighter and Hercules admired her skill. She jumped at him with her spear and Hercules had to defend[2] himself. He wrestled her down to the ground and made her give him the jewel-covered-dress.

Hercules left the island with great sadness in his heart. Hippolyte was the strongest woman he had ever met; he had deep love and respect for her. Hercules was angry at Eurystheus' daughter Admete for her terrible greed[3] and desire for the Amazon queen's dress.

---

① **transform** /træns'fɔ:m/ *vt.* 使改变外观

② **defend** /dɪ'fend/ *vt.* 防御；保护；保卫

③ **greed** /gri:d/ *n.* 贪心；贪婪

The Golden Apples

Over the next years, Hercules completed many more tasks for King Eurystheus. He killed the poison birds of Stymphalus①; he wrestled the mad bull of Crete②; he brought the king the wild horses of Diomedes③ and the cows of Geryones; he even traveled to land of the dead and brought the king the three-headed dog that guarded its gates.

Hercules only needed to complete one more task before he was free from his slavery. King Eurystheus thought of the hardest task he could in hopes that Hercules would not be able to complete it. The king gave his last order:

"I want the golden apples that Zeus gave Hera. The apples are guarded by four women, called the

① **Stymphalus** 专指希腊神话中一种有毒的鸟。

② **Crete**【希腊】克里特岛，位于地中海东部。

③ **Diomedes**【希神】狄俄墨得斯，为荷马史诗所描述的特洛伊战争中希腊的一个英雄。

Hesperides[1]. Find the apples and bring them to me!"

This last task seemed impossible! Hercules did not know how to do it. The Hesperides were powerful immortals who would never let Hercules approach the apples. Also, Hercules knew that the Hesperides lived with a great dragon that had teeth as long as swords and could breathe fire so hot that it would melt metal.

After much thinking, Hercules decided that he needed the help of the Titans. The Titans were giant men that had lived in the world before ordinary men were created. Hercules went to find the Titan called Prometheus. Long ago, when the first man was born, Prometheus stole some fire from the gods and gave it as a gift to men. This angered the gods greatly and they punished Prometheus in a terrible way. They tied him with chains to the top of a mountain where a giant meat-eating bird lived. Each day this bird flew down and slowly ate out Prometheus' liver[2]. This was horribly painful. Then, each night,

① **Hesperides**【希神】看守金苹果园的四姊妹。传说赫斯珀里得斯姊妹四仙女与一条龙一起看守长有金苹果的花园。传说西方极乐群岛位于地球的西边，是长有金苹果的花园。

② **liver** /'lɪvə/ *n.* 肝脏

his liver would grow back, so that he would have to go through the same pain the next day.

Hercules climbed the mountain where Prometheus lived. As he climbed, he heard Prometheus' terrible screams and he felt great pity for the Titan. Once on top, Hercules took his bow and arrow and shot the vulture① that had caused Prometheus so much pain over thousands of years. He then broke the chains on Prometheus' hands and feet.

"You have freed me," said Prometheus. "If there is anything I can do to thank you, I will."

"I have also not been free for a long time," said Hercules. "I will not be free until I get the golden apples that Zeus gave Hera."

"Go and see my brother, Atlas②," said Prometheus. "Tell him what you have done for me and he will help you."

Atlas was the largest and the strongest of the Titans. It was his job to carry the earth on his shoulders and kept it separate from③ the heavens.

When Hercules arrived at the place where

① **vulture** /ˈvʌltʃə/ *n.* 兀鹫

② **Atlas**【希神】阿特拉斯（受罚以双肩掮天的巨人）；【喻】身负重担的人。

③ **separate from** 分开；区别

Atlas stood, he looked up at the great Titan and said, "Great Atlas, you keep the earth and heavens apart and all men admire your strength. I have recently freed your brother, Prometheus, from his chains. He told me that you would help me in my current[①] task."

Hercules then told Atlas all about his twelve tasks and about bringing the golden apples to King Eurystheus. "I can certainly help you with your task," said Atlas, "but I cannot leave my job here; I must keep the earth apart from the heavens."

"Perhaps I could hold up the earth for you while you are gone." said Hercules.

"Perhaps you could. Come here and try!" said the Titan.

Atlas slowly lowered the earth down onto Hercules' shoulders. The earth's weight was great, but Hercules was able to support it. When Atlas saw that Hercules was holding the earth firmly, he ran off to find the golden apples.

Atlas returned just a day later with the apples. Because of his great size, he was able to run

---

① **current** /'kʌrənt/ *adj.* 当前的；现在的

to the place where the Hesperides lived in just a few hours. He had killed the dragon while the Hesperides slept and taken the apples easily. However, while he was away, Atlas realized that he was very tired of carrying the earth on his shoulders. He decided that he would not take it back from Hercules. He decided to trick Hercules into holding it forever.

"I have returned with the apples, Hercules," said Atlas, "but I wish to help you more. I will take the apples myself to King Eurystheus for you."

Now Hercules was not a fool. He guessed that Atlas might never come back to carry the earth again. He said, "You are too kind, great Atlas. It would be very helpful if you would take the apples to King Eurystheus. But will you do one thing before you go? I am not used to carrying the earth like you are. It is uncomfortable on my back. If you could just hold the earth for a minute, then I will get my blanket and put it on my back, so that the earth does not hurt me anymore as I hold it."

Atlas agreed and took the earth off Hercules' back and put it on his own. However, Hercules did not go and get his blanket, but instead picked up the golden apples. "I have changed my mind, Atlas. Actually I will take the apples to King Eurystheus myself."

Atlas looked very sad, but did not say anything. He did not want to admit that he was trying to trick Hercules.

When Hercules returned with the apples, Eurystheus was so impressed that he could not feel jealous of his cousin any longer. "You have completed my twelve tasks, Hercules, and done as the gods ordered. You are welcome to stay in my kingdom as long as you want, but not as a slave—you are now a free man."

Hercules left his cousin and the land of Argos soon after and wandered the lands freely again. He traveled to many towns and did many good deeds. He earned great fame for his adventures and had many happy days. Still sadness always lived in his heart, for he could never forget the face of his sweet wife and loving children.

Pygmalion's Statue

On the island of Cyprus[①] lived a man called Pygmalion[②]. Pygmalion was a sculptor, and many people said that he was the best sculptor in the world. He made most of his money by making statues for the many temples on the shores of Cyprus. He was a successful man and lived in one of the largest houses in his village, but he was alone. All of the mothers of the island wanted to marry their daughters off to him because he was both famous and rich. The young women of the island would often visit Pygmalion's house and bring him gifts, but Pygmalion was very particular. He was never pleased with the women he met, and thought they were not beautiful and perfect enough for him. All the young women on the island had tried to win him as a husband, but he rejected them all. This made the women upset. Why didn't this man want to marry and start a family? There wasn't anything

① **Cyprus**（地中海东部一岛）塞浦路斯

② **Pygmalion**【希神】皮格马利翁，塞浦路斯雕刻之王，热恋自己雕的少女像。

wrong with them! One day, all the young women of Cyprus went to the temple of Aphrodite, the goddess of love, and prayed that Pygmalion would take a wife. High up in heaven, Aphrodite heard their prayers and decided to answer their wishes.

One night after a hard day's work, Pygmalion got into bed. Moonlight came in through his window and filled the room with soft light. Suddenly he heard a voice, but could see no person. It was the most beautiful voice he had ever heard. "You have upset the women of this island, Pygmalion," it said.

Pygmalion jumped out of bed, and the goddess Aphrodite appeared before him. She was tall and light seemed to come from inside her. She was so beautiful that Pygmalion could hardly breathe. As he looked at her, his body felt like it was on fire. He sat staring at the goddess before him and did not move or speak.

"The women of the island have prayed to me—they wish you to take a wife. In answer to their prayer, I will make this so, but since you are a great artist and have always honored the gods, I will let you choose any woman you want. Any woman on this island shall be yours; you need only say her name."

Pygmalion tried to speak, but his voice was not much louder than a whisper because of his wonder at the goddess. "I have no desire for a wife."

Aphrodite sat down on one knee and looked deep into his eyes. As he looked into her eyes, he understood what true love was for the first time in his life. Then Aphrodite spoke again, "You are being given a gift that no other man has had, Pygmalion. You may choose any woman, and she will be yours."

Pygmalion could not say "no" to the goddess, but he could not imagine taking a wife now that he had seen the beauty of Aphrodite. Suddenly, he had an idea, "I will choose a wife," he said, "but first I wish to complete one last statue. When it is finished, I shall make my choice."

Aphrodite smiled and again Pygmalion's heart felt like it was on fire. "You may create your last statue; I will return when it is complete."

Aphrodite then turned to leave, but Pygmalion stopped her. "Wait! Please, goddess, I wish that you model for my statue. All the beautiful things in the world together are still not as beautiful as you. I want this last statue to be the greatest I have ever made; I wish it to be the most beautiful thing created by a man's hands."

Aphrodite was pleased to hear such sweet words and nodded her head. "I will model for you, Pygmalion. I will return here every night at this time until the statue is complete. When it is finished, I will hear your choice for a wife."

Aphrodite then kissed Pygmalion's forehead and disappeared. Her kiss made his whole body feel warm. When he turned around towards his bed, a single red rose lay on his pillow①.

Aphrodite returned the next evening as she had promised, and the two of them began to work on the statue. Pygmalion began by making small models of the goddess sitting before him. Night after night, Aphrodite came and more small models were made. Soon there were one hundred models; each one was amazing and beautiful. There seemed to be a part of the goddess in every one of them; the shape② and expression of each one was perfect.

① **pillow** /ˈpɪləʊ/ *n.* 枕头

② **shape** /ʃeɪp/ *n.* 形状；身材

Aphrodite was very pleased with all of the models. "I wish to give you a gift, Pygmalion," she said and disappeared.

Aphrodite first went to see Hephaestus, the god of metal, and asked him to make tools from the strongest metals that would always be sharp. Having done this, she then flew to see the goddess of the earth, Gaia[①], and asked for the purest piece of rock that existed in any part of the world. The earth goddess gave it to her and Aphrodite brought it to Pygmalion. It was placed in the center of his house.

"You may now begin your last statue, Pygmalion," Aphrodite whispered in his ear. "I shall return when it is finished." The goddess then disappeared.

Once the goddess was gone, Pygmalion picked up his new tools and began working. First he made a basic model of the statue by removing all of the unnecessary pieces of rock. Then he began working on the smaller pieces. He worked all through the night; the hammer was like a part of his arm and every cut he made was strong and true. Even

① **Gaia**【希神】盖亚（大地女神）。

though every muscle in his body began to hurt, he kept working. An entire week passed, during which Pygmalion only stopped working to eat and sleep for short periods.

After this week, the statue was finally done. He stepped back and stared at his work to see if there were any places that needed to be improved. There were none; his work was perfect! He stood with his mouth open, unable to take his eyes off the beauty of the stone woman he had made. Her arms were reaching out, as if they were searching for a person to hold. She was not wearing any clothes, and her body was only covered by her extremely long hair. When Pygmalion finally turned away from the statue, he saw Aphrodite standing there.

"It is truly beautiful, Pygmalion. I am very pleased." She smiled. "Now it is time that you chose a wife."

Pygmalion stepped forward: "I chose her, my statue." He stepped up to the statue and put his arms around the rock. "This woman is the only thing that I shall ever be able to love. If I cannot have her in life, then I wish to become rock as well and stand in her arms for the rest of time." Pygmalion looked into the statue's eyes and kissed the cold stone lips.

Aphrodite's heart was moved by his words. She picked up the red rose that she had left her first night in Pygmalion's house and touched it to the hair of the statue. Suddenly, the lips of the statue became warm beneath① Pygmalion's, and the hard arms bent and held him. What was once cold, hard stone was now warm flesh② and blood! Aphrodite had given him the love that he had chosen, thus fulfilling③ her promise.

"I have given you your wish, Pygmalion. Before you stand your true love, a piece of your own work, your art. Be good to each other and forever remember this gift I have given each of you." Aphrodite then smiled and disappeared.

Pygmalion stared at his new wife with eyes full of tears. She smiled back at him with a smile just like Aphrodite's.

---

① **beneath** /bɪˈniːθ/ *prep.* 在……的下方

② **flesh** /fleʃ/ *n.* 肉；肉体

③ **fulfill** /fʊlˈfɪl/ *vt.* 实现，履行

The Great Hero Perseus

The Birth of Perseus

In the land of Argos lived a king named Acrisius[①]. Acrisius was a good king and was respected by all the people of the land. King Acrisius had been unlucky, however, because he had only one child, a daughter. Her name was Danae[②] and she was both beautiful and kind. When Danae reached the age of thirteen, Acrisius took her to a blind man who could see the future to ask what was in her fate. The blind man told Acrisius that his daughter would give birth to a great hero. This pleased the king greatly and he asked the blind man to tell him more. "Be warned," said the blind man to the king, "that your daughter's son will one day murder you!"

Upon[③] hearing this, King Acrisius became greatly angry and pulled out his knife to kill his

① **Acrisius**【希神】阿克里西俄斯，阿尔戈斯国王，是达娜厄的父亲，后为自己的外孙珀耳修斯杀死。

② **Danae**【希神】达娜厄，Argos 国王之女，珀耳修斯之母。

③ **upon** /ə'pɒn/ *prep.* 当……时候

daughter. But when he looked into his daughter's eyes, his heart was filled with a father's love and all his anger disappeared. "I cannot kill my own daughter," he thought, "but I must make sure that she never gives birth to a son."

Upon returning to the capital city, King Acrisius ordered his builders① to make a tall tower out of strong metal. When the tower was finished, he locked Danae in the room at the top and ordered that no men ever go near the tower. The king was a wise man and kept the only key to the room, in case② any of the guards became interested in his daughter's beauty.

For the next year, not a single person entered Danae's room. Each day a young servant girl would come and put food through a small window for Danae to eat, but no other person ever entered the tower. One day, the young servant girl heard a sound coming from the room. It was the sound of a baby crying! The servant girl could not believe what she had heard and ran down to tell the king.

When the king heard the news, he was so

① **builder** /ˈbɪldə/ *n.* 建筑者，建立者

② **in case** 免得；以防

shocked that he ran up to the top of the tower and threw open the strong metal door. Inside sat Danae holding a young baby boy in her arms!

"How is this possible?" demanded the king. "Tell me which man has come in here and I will cut off his head myself!"

At this point Danae told the king an amazing story. "Father, it was no man who came in here. The first night you locked me in the tower, I was so lonely that I cried and cried and could not stop. The king of the gods, Zeus, heard my sad tears and came into the room to comfort① me. He came back each night and soon we fell in love. I agreed to marry him secretly and many nights we lay together in my bed. My son, this boy you see here in my arms, is named Perseus②, and he is the son of a god."

King Acrisius did not know whether to believe his daughter or not. Yet, certainly, there was no way into the tower for an ordinary man. "Perhaps," the king thought, "this child is the son of Zeus."

The king did not know what to do. He felt great

---

① **comfort** /ˈkʌmfət/ *vt.* 安慰；抚慰

② **Perseus**【希神】珀耳修斯，宙斯和达娜厄（Danae）之子，杀死女怪美杜莎（Medusa）的神。

love for his daughter, and great respect and fear for the god Zeus. But he remembered the words of the old man, and was afraid that his grandson would one day murder him. In the end, fear won in the king's heart and he decided to kill both Danae and Perseus. Yet the king did love his daughter, so this was a terribly hard decision for him to make. He told his men to lock his daughter and her son in a heavy box and throw them in the sea. The king himself watched all this happen and cried as he watched the box sink into the deep water.

Yet it was not Zeus's wish that his wife and son should die. He called on Poseidon①, the god of the sea, and told him to protect the box under the water. Once the king and his men left, the box again floated to the top of the water and moved towards the island of Serapis.

① **Poseidon**【希神】波塞冬（海神），波塞冬掌管海洋、地震及马匹的神，是宙斯的兄弟。

Dictys' Discovery

The island of Serapis was ruled by a king named Polydectes[①]. Polydectes had a younger brother named Dictys[②] who was fond of[③] the ocean and spent many hours each day sitting on the beach and fishing. He had heard that some of the fish in the ocean were magical, and if caught, they could give men great gifts. He wanted to catch one.

One afternoon, while staring off into the ocean and waiting for a fish to bite, Dictys saw a strange object far out in the water. He watched it for a while and saw that it was moving towards the beach. With a great feeling of excitement, he waited for the object to reach the shore. When it came close, Dictys could see that it was a large wooden box and hoped that there might be some great treasure inside.

① **Polydectes**【希神】波利得特克斯国王（a king of Seriphus），本想娶达娜厄为妻，但珀耳修斯利用美杜莎（Medusa）妖怪头颅的特殊作用使他变成了石头。

② **Dictys**【希神】狄克提斯，塞拉皮斯岛国王波利得特克斯（Polydectes）的弟弟。

③ **be fond of** 喜爱，爱好

He was surprised when he opened the box and found a beautiful young woman and baby inside. "This is a great treasure, indeed," thought Dictys. "I must bring this young lady to meet my brother, the king!"

When King Polydectes saw Danae, he fell in love with her immediately and promised himself that she would one day be his bride.

"This lady came to our island in a wooden box, which floated here over the sea," said Dictys.

Danae bowed to the king.

"Beautiful young girl," began the king, "you do not need to bow to me. You are welcome in my land and will be treated like a part of my family. Your child also, I will raise① him as if he were my own son. You will never lack② food or safety and do not need to worry about your old land and old life anymore."

Danae thanked the king and began her life on the island of Serapis. Everything she wanted was given to her and her life was quite happy. Her life was not perfectly happy though, because after one

① **raise** /reɪz/ *vt.* 养育

② **lack** /læk/ *vt.* 缺乏，不足

year on the island, during the New Year's Festival, the king asked Danae to marry him.

"Oh, great king," said Danae, "I cannot marry you. I am married already to the god Zeus."

At hearing this, king Polydectes became very angry. "Have I not treated you and your son like a part of my family, showing you every kindness and giving you everything you ask?"

"Yes, my king," Danae answered.

"Your husband, Zeus, is not here now and will never come. Certainly he wishes you to marry a man of this earth and be happy. Why will you not marry me?" the king tried to persuade① Danae.

"It is too soon, my king. Only when I am sure that Zeus will not return for me, will I agree to marry you," said Danae.

"When will you be sure of that?" the king asked.

"In twenty more years," answered Danae, "if he has not come for me by then, I will marry you."

Truthfully, Danae did not want to marry Polydectes at all. She both loved Zeus and feared

① **persuade** /pəˈsweɪd/ *vt.* 说服；劝说

his anger. But she knew that if she didn't agree to marry the King sometime[1], he might become jealous and hurt her or Perseus in his anger.

King Polydectes was not at all pleased by Danae's answer, for he did not want to wait twenty years to marry her. But there was nothing else he could do, so he agreed to wait anyway. "Lovely Danae, I will wait twenty years to take you as my bride. Still, I will ask you to marry me each New Year's Festival—just in case you have changed your mind."

① **sometime** /ˈsʌmtaɪm/ *adv.* (≠ sometimes) 在某时；有朝一日，例：It happened sometime last month. 此事发生在上月的某个时候。sometime *adj.* 曾经是……的；从前的；昔日的，例：Mr. X, the sometime professor of physics. X 先生，前任物理学教授。

Given a Dangerous Task

As the years passed by, Perseus grew into a strong and brave man. He had the blood of Zeus in him and received kind treatment and love from his mother and King Polydectes as well.

In the king's mind, Danae became more beautiful each year. Every New Year's Festival, his requests to marry her became stronger and stronger. Already eighteen years had passed, and in only two years Danae would have to become his bride.

Perseus knew that his mother did not want to marry Polydectes and wanted to protect her from the king. With the goal of his mother's happiness in his mind, Perseus went to see the king and speak with him.

"Polydectes, my mother has told me that you have asked her to marry you once again. For eighteen years she has refused you. Don't you understand that she is married already, to the greatest of gods? Why don't you leave her alone[①]?"

① **leave sb. alone** 不干涉 / 不理会某人

"You are acting quite rudely," said Polydectes, "my future marriage to your mother is not your affair!"

Hearing this, Perseus stood up to his full height and pointed his finger at Polydectes. "If you try to bother my mother at the next New Year's Festival, then you will have to deal with me! Unless you kill me first, I will not let you have her as your bride."

"You speak of great violence, young man. When I was young, I would never dare say such terrible words to people older than me. Certainly, I would not speak this way to a man who had raised me with every kindness and acted as my loving father. I understand your mind, young Perseus. You wish to prove that you are a strong man and a brave fighter. Do not start a fight with me. Find a real enemy instead! Kill them to prove that you are now a man."

"I have only one enemy on this island," began Perseus, "the man who would force my dear mother to marry him! There are no other terrible monsters for me to fight here."

Polydectes pulled out his sword and handed it to Perseus. "Go out into the world and find a great enemy. There are monsters all over the land that need to be killed."

Perseus was interested in the king's words. "Name any great monster and I will bring you their heads!"

King Polydectes did not have the youth and strength to defeat① Perseus and feared that Perseus would try to stop his wedding. Because of this, he tried to name the most terrible and dangerous monster that he could. "This monster will surely kill Perseus for me," the king thought.

"Perseus, if you wish to be known as a great hero, you should kill the monster called Medusa②," the king said with an honest face, hiding his terrible thoughts. "You are so strong and brave. I am sure you can kill her without much trouble!"

"Who is this Medusa and where can I find her?" Perseus asked.

"She lives in the lands north of here," said Polydectes. "Now go and prove that you are a hero!"

① **defeat** /dɪˈfiːt/ *vt.* 击败，战胜

② **Medusa**【希神】美杜莎，被珀耳修斯所杀的蛇发女怪，长有蛇发、令人恐怖的女妖。

The Goddess Athena

Perseus left the palace and walked along the beach, staring out across the sea to the north. In his heart, he was sad and worried. He wished to prove that he was a great hero, but he did not know about this Medusa, where to find her, or how to defeat her. As he stood looking out at the water, a beautiful woman approached① him carrying a shield②, helmet③, and pair of boots.

As the woman came closer, she seemed to be surrounded by a bright light and Perseus could not look directly at her.

"Certainly you are a goddess," Perseus said and bowed down low to the ground.

"Stand up, my child," said the goddess. "I am the goddess Athena; I have come to bring you three gifts."

"So you know of the adventure I have ahead?" said Perseus.

① **approach** /ə'prəʊtʃ/ *vt.* 接近，靠近

② **shield** /ʃi:ld/ *n.* 盾，盾形物

③ **helmet** /'helmɪt/ *n.* 头盔，防护帽

"Yes, my child. Do not fear Medusa, because the gods will help you. Hades, god of the underworld, has sent you this helmet. When wearing this helmet, you will be invisible① to human eyes. Apollo, the voice② of the gods, has sent you these magic boots. With these boots on you can fly like a bird. Lastly, I have made you a special shield that is made from a pure metal and works like a mirror. This shield is perhaps the most important gift. You will need it to complete your task."

"Oh, great Athena, thank you for these kind gifts. I am sure, with the gods protecting me, that I will not fail to kill Medusa. But, can you tell me more about Medusa? I do not even know what it is that I must fight!" Perseus looked troubled.

"To learn more about Medusa," said Athena, "go and visit the three blind sisters in the island north of here."

Athena then disappeared, leaving Perseus alone on the beach.

---

① **invisible** /ɪnˈvɪzəbl/ *adj.* 无形的，看不见的

② **voice** /vɔɪs/ *n.*=**A medium or an agency of expression** 喉舌，代言人，表达的中介或媒介。

The Three Blind Sisters

The very next morning, Perseus said goodbye to his mother and went to find the three blind sisters. The three blind sisters had lived for hundreds of years and knew many secret things that others did not know. Perseus had heard many terrible stories about them. It was said that they were so old that they only had one tooth and one eye left between them and they had to share them. Because they only had one tooth, they had to spend most of the day eating slowly. Because they only had one eye, it was hard to find food, and they often ate men who came asking them questions.

Perseus put on his flying boots and helmet of invisibility and flew towards the mountain where the three blind sisters lived. As he flew over the ocean, he feared that his boots would stop working and that he would fall into the sea, but the boots were a gift from Apollo himself, and they carried him across the sea safely. Once Perseus was on land, no one saw him for he was wearing his helmet of invisibility.

He climbed the mountain of the three blind sisters and entered the cave where they lived. Immediately the sisters smelled him, because, without eyesight, their power of smell was sharp.

"I smell something. What is it? It smells juicy and good. I'm hungry!" said the youngest sister.

"It is a man," said the middle sister.

"Quickly, give me the eye!" said the oldest sister.

Perseus watched as the oldest sister reached into the middle sister's head and pulled out the one eye. She then pushed the eye into her own head and looked around the room. Perseus was still wearing his helmet, however, and the old sister could not see him.

"Yes, it's a man; I hear a man's footsteps on the rock floor; yet, I see no one!" the old sister said angrily. "Where are you hiding, young man?"

"I have come to ask you about Medusa," said Perseus in a strong voice.

"We will tell you nothing!" yelled the three sisters together. "Not until we can see you."

The other two sisters came close to the oldest so that they would not be far from the eye that they depended on.

The youngest sister spoke:

"Give me the eye, sister, I am younger than you and can see better with it. I will find this young man!"

Perseus watched as the youngest sister pulled the eye out of the oldest sister's head. Just when she was about to put it in her own head Perseus grabbed it out of her hand.

"Our eye, he stole our eye!" shouted the young sister.

"Give it back, you thief ! We'll make you sorry, we will!" all three sisters said with voices like snakes.

Perseus laughed at the sisters. "Oh, I think I will keep your eye, since you will not answer my questions about Medusa. I will see you later, but I don't think you will see me."

"Wait! Come back!" cried the sisters. "Oh, all right! We will tell you what you want to know."

"Very well," said Perseus, "tell me about this monster called Medusa."

The middle sister answered his question with great hatred in her voice. "Long ago, Medusa was once a beautiful woman with two sisters. Medusa was very vain, and she told her sisters that she was more beautiful than even the goddess Athena, and her sisters agreed with her. Of course Athena heard what Medusa had said and was very angry. She decided to punish them all. She changed Medusa and her sisters into Gorgons[①]—the most terrible and ugly monsters on this earth. They have the body of a woman, but their legs have become snakes. Also, Medusa's long, beautiful hair was turned into a group of snakes as well. She is the most horrible looking of them all! Her face is so ugly that if anyone looks into her eyes, they will be changed into stone. The only way to look at her is by using a mirror."

"So that is why Athena gave me this mirror shield," thought Perseus.

"Where can I find this monster?" demanded Perseus.

"She lives with her sisters on the Island of the Gorgons, far to the north of here. Just follow the north wind and you will find it."

① **Gorgon**【希神】戈尔贡，斯塞诺、尤里安勒和人形的可怕的美杜莎三姐妹中的任何一个，美杜莎以毒蛇为头发，凡看到她眼睛的人都会变为石头。指丑陋的或令人厌恶的女人。

Hearing this, Perseus turned to leave and threw the eye down on the floor. The three old women jumped down on the floor, feeling around for their precious eye.

The Gorgon Medusa

Perseus left the cave and flew straight to the Island of the Gorgons. He searched the island for Medusa and found her sleeping next to her two sisters. They were truly as horrible as Perseus had been told. Their bodies were not pink like humans, but green like a snake; their hair, which was all snakes, seemed to fight with itself; and the air was thick with their terrible smell.

Very quietly, Perseus walked up to Medusa's sleeping body, pulled out his sword, and prepared to cut off her head. Just then, her snake hair woke up and hissed① at him. The three Gorgons awoke and Perseus quickly turned around so that he would not see Medusa's eyes and be turned into stone.

The horrible monsters jumped at Perseus, but he avoided② their terrible arms with his quick steps. He used the inside of his shield, which was as clear as a mirror, to watch out for the Gorgons as he

① **hiss** /hɪs/ *vi.* 发出"嘶嘶"声

② **avoid** /əˈvɔɪd/ *vt.* 避开，避免

ran into a forest nearby. The three women carried bows and arrows and hunted him in the woods.

After finding a safe place to hide, Perseus had an idea how to kill Medusa. He hung his shield on a tree and then hid behind another tree nearby. He moved his body so that his face was reflected[①] in his shield and waited for Medusa to see it. When Medusa noticed his face in the shield, she thought it was him and jumped at it. Just then, Perseus came up behind her and, with one strong movement of his arms, cut off her head.

Perseus knew that Medusa's head was still very dangerous and did not look down at it. Instead he used his shield as a mirror, reached down behind him, picked up the head, and put it into his bag. He then closed his bag and flew off the island.

① **reflect** /rɪˈflekt/ *vt.* 反映，照出（如在水中或镜中）

The Titan Atlas

After flying for a while, Perseus came near the great Titan, Atlas. The gods had ordered Atlas to keep the sky and the earth apart for all of time. So for centuries Atlas had held the weight of the earth on his shoulders. When the Titan saw Perseus, he cried out to him.

"Great flying hero! Please come and talk with me a while; I am so tired and lonely here for nobody ever stops to speak with me."

Perseus respected the Titan for his difficult work and agreed to stop for a while. When Perseus told Atlas about killing Medusa, the Titan became very excited. "Is it true that anyone who looks at her face will be turned into stone?" he asked.

"It is true, great Titan," answer Perseus.

"Then please let me see it!" Atlas begged.

"Why would you wish to see it?" asked Perseus, "even one so large and powerful as you would turn to stone."

Atlas let out a long, deep breath. "I have carried this heavy world on my shoulders for a longer time than I can remember. I never eat, nor sleep, and never receive a rest from my pain. No people come to see me, and I suffer alone. Still, the gods have asked me to do this, and I cannot say no. If you would show me the head of Medusa and change me into stone, then I could end my suffering without dropping the world off my shoulders."

Perseus felt deep sorrow for the suffering of the Titan. He agreed to do what Atlas asked. He took out his bag and reached for the Medusa's head.

"Goodbye, dear Earth, goodbye, sweet Heavens; I have done what I promised, and I will continue to keep you apart forever."

Perseus pulled Medusa's head out of the bag and turned his own head away. The Titan did not look at Medusa in fear, but smiled at her with happiness. A moment later he was changed into stone. When Perseus turned around, he saw a huge mountain sitting where Atlas once stood.

Andromeda and the Sea Monster

As Perseus flew back toward the island of Serapis, he happened to see a very strange sight. A young woman was tied to a large rock out in the sea. Perseus flew close to the rock and saw that the woman was very beautiful and also very afraid. She did not seem to see Perseus and stared out at the sea in front of her with a look of fear in her eyes.

Perseus flew down and landed on the shore near the rock. There was a large group of men and women watching the young woman and the sea. All of the women were crying, and the men had sad eyes as well.

Perseus walked up to the man in front of the group and asked angrily, "Why is that young woman tied to that rock? Who has done such a terrible thing?"

"I tied her there," said the man, "but do not call me a cruel man, for truly I am the saddest father in the world. I am the king of this island, and that young girl, Andromeda[①], is my only daughter."

"Why have you tied her out there?" asked Perseus.

The king answered with dark eyes and a slow, sad voice. "Each month, a terrible sea-monster comes to this island and takes away[②] many of our children. I have learned from a wise old man, one who knows about the monsters of the sea, that the only way to stop this monster is to give him my daughter. So, to protect my people, I have put my daughter out on that rock."

Just then[③], large waves began to hit the beach[④] and a large head appeared out of the water. Slowly, the sea-monster stood up to its full height of twenty meters and approached the beach. All the people screamed in fear as they saw the monster's large, black eyes and sharp, white teeth. It had a long tail which made great waves every time it hit the water.

When Perseus heard Andromeda scream, he

---

① **Andromeda**【希神】安德洛墨达是刻甫斯和卡西奥佩娅的女儿，其丈夫珀耳修斯曾把她从海妖手里救出。

② **take away** 带走，抓走

③ **just then** 就在这时候，那时候

④ **hit the beach**【美俚】【航海】登陆上岸

jumped into the air and flew at the sea-monster with his sword in his hand. The monster tried to hit Perseus down with his large hand, but Perseus flew too quickly and avoided each attack. Then, flying forward as fast as he was able, Perseus pushed his sword into the monster's neck. The sea-monster let out a horrible scream and blood poured out of its mouth. Its great body then fell down, creating a huge wave as it hit the water. The wave rose up out of the ocean, as tall as a building.

Perseus was fast and smart and knew what was about to happen. Before the great wave reached Andromeda, Perseus had untied her and flew her to safety. The men and women on the shore all clapped their hands together and thanked Perseus for his great deed.

"Young hero," said the king, "I do not know who you are, but we all thank you for your brave help. You have saved this land and you have saved my daughter from a horrible death! If there is anything in my kingdom that you would like as a reward, you may certainly have it."

"If I may have anything," began Perseus, "then

I would like to take your fair daughter, Andromeda, as my wife."

"If that would please you, great hero, then I give her to you with the greatest happiness," said the king.

Perseus then turned to Andromeda and sat down on one knee. "I cannot take your daughter unless she, too, agrees. Will you marry me, lovely Andromeda?"

Andromeda walked over to Perseus and reached out her hand to him. He looked up into her eyes and kissed her hand softly. A great cheer of excitement came from the crowd and, right then and there[①], Perseus and Andromeda were married.

① **right then and there** 当时，当场 right = exactly

Stopping an Unwanted Wedding

Perseus did not stay long on this island, for he needed to return home. It had been twenty years since Danae and Perseus were found by Dictys, and soon his mother would have to marry King Polydectes. Andromeda's father gave him a boat, and with his new wife he sailed back to Serapis.

They arrived just a day before the wedding. Perseus went first to see his mother. She was sitting in her room crying. "Oh[①], my son," she said, "tomorrow I must marry Polydectes. I know that Zeus will be angry and bring terrible things to this island. Tonight I will kill myself, so that I do not have to wed[②]."

"No, mother," said Perseus, "I will go see Polydectes and change his mind. You must promise me not to kill yourself tonight."

Before going to see the king, Perseus carefully

① **oh** /əʊ/【叹词】啊，嗬，唉，呀，噢……用以表达强烈情感，如惊讶、害怕、愤怒或痛苦；用于直接对人讲话或表示对于陈述的理解或认同。

② **wed** /wed/ *vi.* 结婚

put Medusa's head in a beautiful box and tied it up to look like a wedding present. He then carried the box in his arms and went to see the king. Entering the king's great hall, Perseus smiled and held out[①] the box to Polydectes and spoke in a friendly voice:

"King Polydectes, tomorrow you will marry my mother at last. How happy you must be! I have brought you a wedding gift to celebrate the event." Perseus handed him the box and bowed low. The king was surprised to see Perseus, for he thought that Medusa would certainly have killed him. "Have you killed the monster, Medusa?" asked the king.

"Yes, I have done exactly as I promised," answered Perseus.

The king was shocked that Perseus had succeeded, but did not want to show his disappointment. He thanked Perseus for the wedding gift and opened the box. Looking inside, he saw Medusa's ugly face staring up at him and was instantly turned into stone.

---

① **hold out** 伸出（手等）；递出

Return to Argos

Soon after killing Polydectes, Perseus decided to take his bride Andromeda and his mother back to his home country. Meanwhile, King Acrisius felt sure that his grandson would never return to kill him, as the fortune-teller[①] had predicted[②]. Surely, he thought, his daughter and grandson had died in the sea twenty years before.

Before Perseus left Serapis, he made Dictys king of the island and thanked him once again for all his kindness. The three arrived in Argos, where Perseus was born, and learned that his grandfather, Acrisius, had gone away for a while. Then, while Perseus was waiting for the king to return, he heard of some athletic[③] games happening in the north. He went north to join the games and hoped to win fame for his skills. His wife and mother waited in Argos for Acrisius' return.

Perseus entered the athletic games but he did

① **fortune-teller** *n.* 给人算命的人；算命先生

② **predict** /prɪˈdɪkt/ *vt.* 预言，预测

③ **athletic** /æθˈletɪk/ *adj.* 运动员的；运动的

not give his name or meet the king and his guests. If he had done so, he might have seen that his grandfather was among them. Acrisius, too, had no idea that one of the athletes was his grandson Perseus.

Perseus won the first two contests, running and jumping, and was admired by all the women and men in the crowd. The third event was the spear throw. When Perseus' turn came, he held the spear perfectly, for he had great experience using one. Then, with great strength, he threw it forward and watched it go straight down the field. But suddenly, the spear changed direction in the air and flew toward the crowd of people watching the games. The sharp head of the spear hit one of the king's guests, who fell down dead.

Perseus ran forward and asked the king why the spear had moved so wildly in the air. The king spoke sadly, "It must have been the wish of the gods." Perseus learned later that the man who had died was Acrisius, his grandfather. He stayed for the funeral and then told the news to Danae and Andromeda. Danae was sad, but the memory of herself and her son cruelly locked in the tower and then thrown in the sea made her feel less bad about her father's death.

Perseus and Andromeda ruled Argos well for many years to come. After their deaths, they were placed in the sky as stars.

King Midas and His Golden Touch

Long ago, Greece was divided into many different small kingdoms. One of these kingdoms was ruled by a man named King Midas①. King Midas was very rich. Many people said that he had more gold than any other king in the world. Even though he was rich, Midas was so greedy that he always wanted to be richer. His favorite thing was gold, and he would do anything to get more. Truly, he wished that everything in his kingdom could be gold, and he hated looking at any object that wasn't. He wore yellow robes and slept in a yellow bed because they reminded him of gold. He even used a golden knife and fork to eat.

Midas loved gold so much that he named his only daughter Marygold. If there was anything that King Midas loved as much as gold, it was his young daughter. She was a beautiful little girl and she loved to play in the castle's garden. Each morning

① **Midas**【希神】迈达斯，传说中的弗里吉亚（Phrygia）国王，酒神 Dionysus（狄俄尼索斯）[罗马神话中的酒神是 Bacchus（巴克斯）] 赐给他一种力量使他能够把他用手触摸的任何东西变成金子。

she would pick flowers and bring them to her father, and each morning her father would say the same thing:

"What beautiful flowers, my daughter. The only thing that could make them more beautiful is if they were gold."

One day, while out playing in the garden, Marygold found an old man sleeping in a bed of flowers. She called to her father, and he came out quickly to see who it was. The man was not an ordinary man; in fact, he was not a man at all. His name was Silenus[①], and he was a Satyr[②]. He was good friends with Dionysus, the god of wine.

When King Midas found Silenus, he did not punish him for destroying his garden. Actually, Midas just laughed at the old man because he was drunk on too much wine. The noise awoke Silenus, and King Midas invited him inside to have dinner and wine. Silenus stayed as the king's guest for ten days, and the two men merrily drank wine and ate

① **Silenus** 西勒诺斯，跟随酒神的塞特，通常被描述为好酒和寻欢作乐之神。在希腊的花瓶上被描绘成带尾巴、耳朵和马蹄的男子和宗教狂欢中庆祝大自然权力与丰产之神。

② **Satyr**【希腊及罗马神话】萨堤尔，半人半兽的森林之神，好色之徒，性欲极强的男人。

great dinners the whole time.

After ten days, Dionysus came to find Silenus. When he arrived at the castle, he found Silenus and Midas walking in the garden.

"So there you are, Silenus," began Dionysus, "have you been enjoying yourself here?"

Silenus told Dionysus what a wonderful time he had been having, and about King Midas' kindness. Dionysus was impressed and decided to reward Midas for his good treatment of Silenus.

"Good King Midas," said Dionysus, "thank you for taking care of my good friend, Silenus. As a reward, I will give you one wish."

Midas only thought about it for a second and said, "I wish that everything I touch be turned into beautiful, yellow gold."

"But Midas, you are the richest king in the world," said Dionysus. "No other man has as much gold as you. Do you truly want more?"

"I may be the richest," said the king, "but I would like much more; for gold is the best and the most wonderful thing in the world."

"Are you sure you will not regret your wish?"

asked Dionysus.

"I am very sure," answered King Midas.

"I will give you your wish then," said Dionysus. "At sunrise tomorrow morning, your touch will turn anything into gold."

The next day Midas awoke very early. He was very excited to use his magic power and make his whole kingdom into gold.

As soon as the sun came up above the mountains, Midas tried his magic power by touching the bed lightly with his hand. Instantly the bed turned into gold. He then walked around the room touching many other things. He touched the chair and table, the mirror hanging on the wall, and all of his clothing—all of them turned into gold.

King Midas was wild with joy. He put on some of his, now gold, clothing and ran around the castle, touching everything he could see. His magic gift turned all into shining, yellow gold. He even ran out into the garden and touched all of the trees and flowers and they all became gold as well.

The king soon felt hungry and went back inside to eat his breakfast. Before sitting down, he touched the table, chairs, and plates, and they all turned into gold. He was so happy that he ordered his cooks to make him a great meal of all his favorite foods. The servants came in carrying many plates of food and King Midas looked out at all the delicious meat and cakes.

Now a strange thing happened. He reached for an egg and put it on his plate. When he looked down, he saw that the egg had turned into gold. He then lifted a glass of clear cold water to drink, but it became gold too. The same thing happened with all of his food: the cakes turned to gold; the meat was hard, and yellow, and shiny. As much as he tried, he could not get anything to eat. It had all become gold, gold, gold!

Just then, Marygold came running in from the garden. She was holding a flower in her hand and crying.

"Why are you crying, my love?" King Midas asked.

"Something terrible has happened to the flowers!" cried Marygold and held up a gold rose.

"Why, there isn't anything wrong with the

flowers," said the king to his daughter, "they are better than before—they are gold!"

Marygold did not care though. "Before the flowers were many different colors and they had a beautiful smell. Now they are all one color and hard and they don't smell at all," she cried.

Midas did not like to see his daughter crying and reached his arms around her and held her tightly. "It will be okay," he said. "Daddy will plant new flowers for you."

Marygold did not answer. When Midas looked down at her, he saw that she, too, had become gold!

Suddenly the king became very afraid. He had lost his daughter, the most wonderful thing in the world to him. Also he knew that he would not be able to eat and would soon die. He put his head down on the table and cried loudly.

"Is something wrong?" asked a voice.

The king looked up and saw Dionysus.

"Oh, great Dionysus, I was wrong," Midas cried. "I do not want the golden touch. Please take away this horrible power! You may have my kingdom and my castle and all of my money; just give

me back my daughter."

"But don't you think that gold is the greatest thing in the world?" asked Dionysus.

"No! I hate it and cannot bear to even look at it!" cried Midas.

"Are you sure that you do not want the golden touch?" asked Dionysus.

"I am sure; I understand better now," said the king. "I now see that gold isn't the greatest thing in the world."

"So you now see that there are things in life more valuable than gold," said Dionysus. "I will take away your golden touch. Take this bucket to the river behind the castle and fill it with water. Pour this water on anything you have turned into gold and it will return to its original state."

King Midas took the bucket and rushed to the river. He returned just a few minutes later and poured the bucket of water on his daughter. Instantly she became flesh again. Midas felt as happy as he had ever felt and held his daughter tightly.

The king then used the water to change back his food and water. He and Marygold sat down together and had a great meal. King Midas was amazed at how good everything tasted and how cold and fresh the water felt.

After breakfast, he and Marygold walked around the castle together changing back everything that he had touched earlier. The only thing that never changed back was Marygold's hair. It had turned from black into golden yellow, and it stayed that way for the rest of her life.

Jason and the Argonauts

A Murdered Father

Iolcus was the king of a great land, and he had only one son, Jason①, who he hoped would rule the land after he died. But the story of Iolcus is an unhappy one, for he never saw his son grow to manhood and stand beside him. Instead, while Jason was still young, the king's brother, Pelias②, killed Iolcus and made himself king of the land. But Pelias was afraid he would lose the land he had violently taken, so he planned to kill Jason as well. But Jason's mother tricked Pelias, pretending that Jason had died from sickness. Meanwhile, she gave her baby son to Chiron③, the Centaur④. Chiron was half man and half horse and was both strong and wise. He taught Jason skills with a sword and much knowledge from great books.

① **Jason**【希神】伊阿宋，为美狄亚（Medea）的丈夫，夺取金羊毛的阿尔戈英雄们的首领。

② **Pelias**【希神】珀利阿斯，伊奥尔科斯（Iolcus）国王的弟弟。

③ **Chiron**【希神】喀戎，博学多智的半人半马怪物，曾是阿喀琉斯（Achilles）、赫拉克勒斯（Hercules）和阿斯克勒庇俄斯（Asclepius）的老师。

④ **Centaur**【希神】人首马身的怪物，半人马座。

When Jason turned sixteen years old and became a man, Chiron told him the story of his father's murder. Immediately Jason left to find Pelias and take back his father's land.

Jason was not Pelias' only enemy. In fact, Pelias had a terrible enemy in heaven among the gods. Jason's uncle, the murderer king, had prayed and given gifts to all the gods except Hera, the wife of Zeus. Because of this, Hera hated King Pelias and wanted to see him lose his power. She decided to test Jason to see if he was a good man who deserved to become king. Hera's test was a dangerous one; only a true hero would pass it.

As Jason walked, Hera caused a great storm to begin. She then turned herself into an old woman and stood beside a fast and terrible river. When Jason saw the old woman, he asked her what she was doing, not knowing that a goddess stood before him.

"There used to be a bridge here," said the old woman, "but now the storm has destroyed it. I need to get home. Would you carry me across the water?"

Now, the storm had caused the river to fill with

water and crossing it would be very dangerous. But Jason did not stop to think about his own safety and carefully picked up the old woman. As he carried her across the river, Hera decided to make the test even harder and made herself heavier and heavier. Jason was strong enough and succeeded in reaching the other side. Hera was impressed with Jason's deed and decided to help him become king.

Pelias' Trick

A few days later Jason arrived at Pelias' castle. Jason was a brave man, but he was young and had a hot heart. He did not fear any man, but he was not yet wise like an old man. Because of this he ran straight into Pelias' castle and demanded, "Pelias, my uncle, I am the son of Iolcus. I have come to become king and rule this land!"

Now, Pelias was not young and strong like Jason, but he had the wisdom of an old king. He did not wish to give up his power and let Jason rule the land. Though he could not beat Jason in a fight, Pelias felt that he could beat him with his mind. He decided to pretend to be friendly to Jason and invited him to eat a great meal.

During the meal, Pelias and Jason had much conversation together. "I am so glad you have come, Jason," said the king. "I am too old to rule, and I need a strong and wise young man to become king after I die. You say that you are able to rule a kingdom, so I am sure that you can handle any difficult problems that appear. For example, how would you go about getting rid of a strong, young man who was giving you difficulties?"

Jason wanted to show Pelias that he was smart and wise enough to fix[1] any problem. "I would send him on a difficult journey—one so difficult that he would never return." he suggested.

"That is a great idea," responded Pelias. "What journey would you send him on?"

"I would ask him to find the Golden Fleece[2]," answered Jason.

"That is a great idea!" said Pelias. "Any true hero would be very excited for that task. If a hero succeeded in finding the Golden Fleece, he would win great fame and all men would sing songs about him."

"Do you think so?" asked Jason. "Then I will go myself to find the Golden Fleece."

"You are truly a brave man," said the king. "If you return, you will deserve to be king and I will give you the kingdom willingly." Pelias laughed to

① **fix** /fɪks/ *vt.* 安排；弄妥

② **Golden Fleece**【希神】金羊毛，金公羊的毛，被伊阿宋和阿尔戈英雄从科尔基斯的国王那里偷走。

himself, because he felt that Jason would certainly die trying to get the Golden Fleece. The fleece was guarded by a large dragon. Also, many dangers would face Jason on the way to the fleece. Surely, Pelias felt, he would not have to give Jason the kingdom.

The Argo and the Argonauts

The day after his conversation with Pelias, Jason began his preparations. The Golden Fleece was owned by King Aeetes, ruler of the land of Colchis①. The journey to Colchis would take many months by ship and Jason knew that only the best of ships would make it safely. Jason hired Argus, the most famous ship builder, and asked him to make the greatest ship of all time. Argus used all of his skill and made a ship that was both fast and strong. Then Hera, who wished to help Jason on his quest, visited Argus and gave him a magical figurehead② to hang on the front of the ship. The figurehead could see the direction of the waves and wind and would warn Jason of storms and other dangers. Argus was so proud of his ship that he gave it his own name and called it the "Argo③."

Jason then searched for companions to help

① **Colchis**【希神】科尔基斯，高加索山脉南面靠近黑海的一个古地区，是传奇中伊阿宋寻找金羊毛的地方。

② **figurehead** /ˈfigəhed/ *n.* 船头雕饰

③ **Argo**【希神】阿尔戈号，伊阿宋乘坐的寻找金羊毛的船。

him in his dangerous task. To accomplish[①] this, he sent messengers to find strong men interested in adventure. From all around Greece, many heroes learned of Jason's journey for the fleece and came to join him. These men were called the Argonauts[②], since they would all sail on the Argo. Among them were Zetes and Calais, who were sons of the North Wind and able to fly; Tiphys, the world's greatest ship sailor; Hercules, the world's strongest man; Hercules' good friend Hylas[③]; and even the great musician Orpheus. They all joined Jason in his great adventure.

Within a month, all of the preparations were made. Jason said goodbye to his uncle and promised to return soon with the fleece. The Argonauts each began their work on the ship and Orpheus played sweet music to cheer them. They sailed for a week before coming to a small island, where they stopped to gather more food and fresh water.

Once the Argonauts were on land they were

① **accomplish** /əˈkʌmplɪʃ/ *vt.* 完成，做成功

② **Argonaut**【希神】阿尔戈（又译亚尔古）英雄，在阿尔戈号与伊阿宋一块儿航行寻找金羊毛的人。

③ **Hylas**【希、罗神】许拉斯，赫拉克勒斯（Hercules）的朋友，是个美丽的男子，被水妖抢走。

quickly surrounded by an army of women. Without knowing it, they had landed① on the island of Lemnos②—an island where the women had joined together and killed all the men. The queen of Lemnos was called Hypsipyle, and she was both beautiful and strong. Hypsipyle felt that men were troublesome and should all be killed, but she changed her mind when she saw how strong and handsome Jason was.

Hypsipyle invited Jason and all the Argonauts to stay on Lemnos. They rested there for more than a month. They spent their days eating great meals and drinking wine. At night, the women would pay great attention to each of them. Jason was so happy lying in Hypsipyle's arms that he never wanted to leave, but finally Hercules convinced him that they should continue their journey.

① **land** /lænd/ *vi.*（使）登岸

② **Lemnos** 利姆诺斯岛（位于希腊）

King Phineus

The next island they reached was called Salmydessus and was ruled by King Phineus. The king welcomed them but was not able to have food prepared for them. Jason noticed that the king was very thin and weak. He told Jason his sad story:

"When I was younger, I did not build any temples to celebrate the gods and did not offer them any food during the year. This made the gods angry and they decided to punish me. They sent three monsters to trouble me; they are called the Harpies① and they have the heads of women and the bodies of birds. The Harpies visit me at every meal and quickly steal my food and go to the bathroom on② my table. Because of this, I can never get enough food to eat and am always becoming thinner and thinner."

① **Harpy** [*pl.* Harpies]【希神】鸟身女怪，有着女人的头和躯干以及鸟的尾巴、翅膀和爪子的可厌的、贪婪的魔怪。

Harpy = A predatory person 掠夺成性的人

Harpy = A shrewish woman 厉害的女人

② **on** /ɔn/ *prep.* 表示接近（to indicate proximity），a town on the border 靠近边界的一个市镇。

Jason felt sorry for the king and promised to help him. He ordered his men, Zetes and Calais, to deal with the Harpies. Zetes and Calais were the sons of the North Wind, and they had the power to fly. When the king next ate, the two brothers hid under his table and waited for the Harpies. Soon, the harpies arrived and grabbed a chicken off of the king's table. Just then, Calais jumped out from under the table, pulled out his sword, and flew after the biggest of the Harpies. The two smaller Harpies went to help their leader and tried to attack Calais from behind. Before they could reach him however, Zetes flew up behind one and pushed his sword through her wing. When the other two Harpies saw their companion fall to the ground, they flew off as fast as they could. Calais chased them until he was sure that they would never come back. They never troubled the king again.

The king was so happy that he ordered the largest party and meal that the island had ever seen. The Argonauts ate and drank until the early hours of the morning. Jason spent the evening telling the king about his quest to find the Golden

Fleece. When the king heard Jason's story, he decided to give him a warning.

"You have scared away the Harpies and brought me much happiness," the king said to Jason. "In thanks, I will tell you how to avoid the next danger you will face. In order to reach the land of Colchis, you will have to sail between two rocks called the Symplegades. These huge rocks wait for ships to pass between them and then quickly close shut—destroying any ship and killing the men inside. No ship is fast enough to pass through safely, but there is a way. Although the Symplegades close very quickly, they open very slowly. Also, they cannot close again until they have first opened all the way back up. If you first send a bird through the Symplegades, they will come together to destroy it. Then, as soon as you see them slowly opening again, you must sail between the two rocks. If your ship is fast and your men are strong, you should be able to make it through before the Symplegades can close a second time."

Jason thanked the king for his wise advice. The next morning, after gathering more food and fresh water, he and the Argonauts set sail again. After traveling a few days they reached the Symplegades. The men stared up at the great rocks with fear in their hearts. Jason ordered his men to row[①] as close to the rocks' edge as they could. He then released a bird that he had caught specifically for this purpose. The two rocks came together with a loud sound, but luckily only the tail feathers of the bird were hurt. The water under the Argo raised and fell from the movement of the great rocks and the men grasped the sides of the ship tightly. When the two rocks began to open again, Jason gave the order, "Row! Row as hard as you can!"

The Argonauts each used all of their strength to row their great ship. The Argo moved forward quickly through the water. The Symplegades opened faster than Jason had expected however, and he saw them preparing to close again. "There is not much time," he yelled. "We must move faster!"

No sooner did he finish speaking, than the rocks began to close together again. "Crash!" went the rocks and Jason heard the sound of breaking

① **row** /rəʊ/ *vi.* 划船

wood. He quickly turned around and saw that the rocks had destroyed only the tail of the boat. They had come through the Symplegades alive!

Losing Hylas

Jason ordered his men to stop at the next island they found to repair the ship. After landing on a small island, everyone set out to find food and fresh water. Hercules and his good friend Hylas went into the forest to cut down trees to get wood to fix the Argo. Though the island did not have any people on it, the two men thought that they heard singing.

The two men went deeper and deeper into the forest, searching for tall and strong trees to cut down. As they walked, the sound of singing grew louder and louder—it was beautiful. Hercules warned Hylas to be careful, "There are many powerful ghosts in this world," he said.

Still, Hylas was curious about the singing and wanted to find out where it was coming from. While Hercules was cutting down a tree, Hylas wandered deeper into the forest until he found a pool of water. He listened closely and it seemed that the singing was coming from deep within the water.

Bending down[1] near the edge of the pool, Hylas stared down into the water. The sound of singing grew stronger, and he saw the faces of three beautiful women rise up under the water. Hylas felt like he was in a dream and reached his hand into the water to touch the beautiful faces. The women put out their hands and held his and sang a soft song that made Hylas feel happy and sleepy. Slowly, they pulled Hylas down into the water.

Hercules had heard the singing change and had run to find his friend. He arrived at the pool just in time to see Hylas' feet sink below the water. Hercules jumped into the pool and searched for[2] his friend, but neither Hylas nor the women could be found.

For two days, Hercules waited by the pool for his friend. Finally, he returned to the Argo and told the other men the sad, strange story. The men had a funeral for Hylas and then left the strange island.

---

① **bend down** 俯身，屈身

② **search for** 搜索，搜寻

The Test

Not many days later, Jason and the Argonauts arrived in Colchis. King Aeetes did not like strangers and wished to have his men kill them all, but when he saw the strength and power of the many heroes, he decided that fighting was not the best way to handle them. Instead the king met with Jason to ask why he had come. When Jason told him about his journey to get the fleece the king grew very angry, but he did not want to start trouble with the Argonauts, so he pretended to be calm.

"You may have the fleece," said the king, "as may any man who passes the test."

"What is the test?" asked Jason.

"Oh, it is simple," lied the king. "There is a large iron plow and two bulls in the field behind my castle. You only need to plow my field and plant my seeds to win the fleece. Oh, and you must plow it in one day."

Jason agreed to the king's request and went

to rest for the next day's test. Of course, the king's test was much harder than Jason knew. The iron plow was too large for any man to lift, and the two bulls had iron feet and breathed fire. They would quickly kill any man that came near them. Also, the seeds that Jason had to plant were not vegetable or fruit seeds. They were seeds that caused huge men with sharp swords to grow out of the ground! The goddess Hera knew that Jason would not be able to complete these tasks alone, and she planned to help him in the night.

King Aeetes had a beautiful daughter named Medea. Late in the evening, Hera persuaded Aphrodite, the goddess of love, to go down to Earth and make Medea fall in love with Jason. Aphrodite agreed and used her magic to fill Medea's heart with love for Jason. Once in love, Medea worried about Jason's safety. She knew that her father had tricked Jason into thinking that the test for the fleece was easy, and she wanted to protect him from any harm.

In the middle of the night, Medea went to see Jason in his room. She told Jason about the difficulties of his test and explained how to pass them.

Just knowing how to pass the test was not enough, however. The bulls were so strong and violent that no ordinary man could use them for work. Fortunately, Medea was good with magic. She created a magic juice that made a man's skin as strong as metal for a day. She told Jason that she would give it to him if he would promise to marry her. Jason promised and thanked Medea for her help.

The next morning Jason and the Argonauts awoke and went to meet with King Aeetes. "Are you ready for your test?" asked the king and handed Jason the bag of seeds that he needed to plant.

Jason had already drunk the magic juice and told the king he was ready. The king led him to his field where many men and women had already gathered to watch Jason try and pass the test. Jason stood in the middle of the field and waited for his enemies.

Soon the two bulls appeared. When they saw Jason, they immediately ran at him with their horns. They hit Jason many times, but each time the attack did not hurt him, thanks to Medea's magic juice. Then, Jason grabbed the first bull and tied the ropes of the plow over his neck. The bull became greatly angry and breathed fire at Jason, but the fire did not hurt him and Jason continued with his task. Soon he had tied the second bull to the plow as well. The people gathered were amazed at the strength of this handsome, young man, and they yelled out in excitement.

Soon Jason had plowed the whole field and began to plant the seeds that the king had given him. As soon as all the seeds were in the ground, each one quickly grew into a powerful soldier with a long sword in his hand. All together, the soldiers moved toward Jason. Now, Jason was not afraid of the soldiers for Medea's magic juice was still protecting him. Still, he knew that he could not defeat so many soldiers by himself. Again, Medea had helped Jason by telling him a way to defeat the army. Jason picked up dirt from the ground and threw it in the eyes of each soldier that came near him. Soon all of the soldiers could not see and they began swinging their swords wildly about them. Within a few hours, the soldiers had all killed one another, and Jason stood alone in the field.

The Golden Fleece

Seeing this angered King Aeetes greatly, "How could he possibly have passed the test?" the king thought. Still, the king had promised to give Jason the fleece if he passed the test. When Jason came over to him, the king spoke cheerfully:

"Truly you are a great hero. Let us celebrate your victory with a great party! Tomorrow I will give you the fleece." In his mind, the king planned to get Jason drunk on wine and kill him while he slept. He asked Medea to help him entertain Jason and the Argonauts at the party, and he told her his plan.

When Medea heard her father's idea, she told Jason about it in secret. "You must get the fleece and escape tonight," she said. "I will take you to get it after tonight's party." During the party, Medea tricked her father by serving Jason and the Argonauts grape juice instead of wine. They did not get drunk and sleepy① as King Aeetes had hoped.

① **sleepy** /ˈsliːpɪ/ *adj.*= **ready for or needing sleep** 想睡的，困的，准备睡眠或需要睡眠的 /asleep = in a state of sleep; sleeping 睡着的，处在睡眠状态的；正睡着的

After the party, Jason ordered the Argonauts to guard the ship. He and Medea went to get the Golden Fleece. When they approached the tree where the fleece was hung, the great dragon guarding it awoke and stood in their way. Medea knew about the dragon and had prepared a special magic medicine. When the dragon smelled the medicine, it fell asleep instantly. Quickly, Jason climbed the tree and put the Golden Fleece in his bag. He and Medea then returned to the Argo and escaped Colchis together.

Early the next morning, the Argo sailed away before King Aeetes realized that either Medea or the fleece was gone. The trip home was easy, and the Argonauts did not face the dangers they had on the way to Colchis. When he returned to his home, Jason became king and married Medea. Jason's story became famous across the kingdom and the Argonauts all became famous as well.

However, the great happiness of Jason and Medea grew less over the years. Jason grew tired of Medea and married a younger and more beautiful princess. Medea was so angry and hurt that she studied more magic and used it to win the love of many great kings. Many kingdoms were destroyed by her evil powers. But these are all stories for another time.

Daedalus and Icarus

Long, long ago in ancient Greece, there lived a famous inventor named Daedalus[①]. Daedalus had invented many machines with many uses. Some of his machines were so amazing that many people felt they were magical.

Since he was famous throughout the country, many kings and rich men would invite him to come to their lands and invent wonderful things to help them with many tasks. On a visit to the island of Crete, the king of the island, King Minos[②], asked Daedalus to build a war machine that would help him to kill his hated enemies. Daedalus was not interested in war and refused to help the king. This angered King Minos greatly, and he ordered that Daedalus be locked up in a high tower that faced the sea until he agreed to do what the king had asked.

Daedalus spent a month in the tower before

① **Daedalus**【希神】代达罗斯（又译第德勒斯），传说中的建筑师和雕刻家，曾为克里特国王建造迷宫。

② **Minos**【希神】迈诺斯（又称弥诺斯），克里特岛之王，宙斯和欧罗巴之子，死后成为地府的三个法官之一。

he was able to escape. His son, named Icarus[①], stole a key from a guard and opened the heavy door of the tower. Daedalus and Icarus ran quickly to the beach and tried to find a ship that would take them back to Greece, but they failed because King Minos had ordered that all ships be carefully searched before leaving the island of Crete. Both Daedalus and Icarus were caught and put in the tower together.

Though he was caught, Daedalus had a strong spirit and felt sure that he could find a way to escape. He thought of inventing something to help them escape, but, unfortunately, there were not many materials in the tower for him to use. After thinking for a long time, he said to his son:

"The King may control the land and the sea, yet he does not control the sky. Therefore, my son, we must escape from the sky!"

Daedalus then told his son to collect all the birds' feathers he could find. Each day the two men would take some of their food and leave it on the opening of the window. When birds came to eat it, they would pull some of their feathers off. Daedalus

① **Icarus**【希神】伊卡洛斯，代达罗斯的儿子，他乘着他父亲做的人工翅膀逃离克里特时，由于离太阳太近以致粘翅膀用的蜡熔化，掉进了爱琴海。

also began saving all the candles that they were given each night.

After many months, Daedalus and Icarus had saved up a lot of feathers and candles, and the inventor began to work. Daedalus melted the candle wax and made it into the shape of wings. He then added the bird feathers until he had built two pairs of wings big enough for him and his son. One pair was large and heavy, big enough for Daedalus; the other pair was small and fast, perfect for Icarus.

When Daedalus had finished the wings, he put them on his back. He began moving his arms up and down and, to Icarus' surprise, began flying around the room. Icarus looked up at his father in amazement. "I want to fly, too," he cried.

Daedalus stopped flying and put the smaller wings on his son. His son's wings, though smaller, were built far better and were more beautiful than his own. Daedalus was proud to give these wings to the son that he loved so much.

The next day was lovely and clear. Daedalus decided it was a good time to teach his son how to fly, so that they could make their escape. He told

Icarus to watch the birds and to fly just like they did. "You must not move your wings too slowly or too quickly, and you must follow the wind."

Icarus put on his wings and jumped out the window of the tower. He then flew up high into the air and dove down low above the sea; he was like a child with a new toy. Daedalus was worried as he watched his son; he knew that the wings were not a toy that one could play with. He called out to his son, and Icarus returned to him.

"Son," he said seriously, "it is time for us to escape this island and return to Greece. As we fly, you must stay close to me always; never fly far away. If you fly too low your wings will become wet from the fog; if you fly too high the wax on the wings will melt from the sun." Icarus smiled and promised his father that he would stay close and be careful.

So Daedalus and Icarus jumped out of the tower window and flew high above the land. The people of Crete looked up in amazement; many people thought they were watching gods flying in the sky. Occasionally Daedalus would turn around to see if his son was still following him closely. For the first hour, Icarus was always just behind his father.

However, a little while later Daedalus looked back and saw that Icarus was not there. Daedalus looked around with great worry in his heart and saw Icarus flying high in the sky. A moment earlier, Icarus had seen two eagles flying above him and became so excited that he decided to follow them. When Icarus felt the cool wind move through his hair, he became even more excited and began to fly faster and faster which made him go higher and higher. Daedalus yelled at his son, “Stop, you are going too high; your wings will melt!” But Icarus was too far away to hear his father. He continued to fly faster and faster, higher and higher, and became more and more excited. Daedalus tried to follow Icarus, but his wings were much heavier. As hard as he tried, he could not reach his son.

The sun began to melt Icarus’ wings, and the feathers slowly began to fall off. Daedalus noticed the wings falling into pieces and tried to scream at his son again, but his son was still too far to hear. Icarus kept flying quickly toward the sun, and his heart became more and more excited. Soon all the feathers had fallen from Icarus' wings and the boy fell down toward the deep sea.

When Daedalus saw his son falling, he flew as fast as he could to catch him. Unfortunately, Daedalus was not fast enough and arrived just a moment too late to save his son. The boy hit the water with a loud, terrible noise. Before Icarus could sink, Daedalus reached into the water and grabbed his leg. He then pulled his son out of the sea and held him closely in his arms. Sadly, it was too late. Icarus had died when he hit the water. Daedalus looked down at the sea and saw the feathers of his son's wings floating on the top of the water. He carried his son's body to a small island and buried it and named the island Icaria in his son's memory①.

Daedalus then put on his wings for one last time and flew back to Greece. In Greece he built a temple to the flying god Apollo and hung up the wings as a promise never to fly again.

① **in one's memory** 为了纪念……

The Story of Theseus

The Birth of Theseus

In the year 1300B.C., a son was born to King Aegeus and his wife, Aethra[①]. He was a fine boy, and they named him Theseus. Just a year earlier, Aegeus had met Aethra in her city of Troezen where she was a princess. For the last year, they had stayed there together; but now King Aegeus had to leave and return to his own kingdom, and it was decided that Aethra would not go with him, but would instead stay in the city where she was born.

King Aegeus was deeply sad about leaving his wife and son, but that was his fortune. Before leaving, he walked around the castle with his wife. Soon they came upon[②] a huge rock and Aegeus used his great strength to lift it. He then dug a small hole where the rock had been, placed his sword and shoes in it and then pushed the rock back over the

① **Aethra**【希神】埃特拉，忒修斯的母亲。

② **come upon** 偶遇

hole. After doing this, he said to his wife:

"My love, I have wished my whole life for a son who would become brave and strong and rule my kingdom when I become old. Raise Theseus into a great man. Do not tell him that his father is a king; instead wait until he is old enough to move this stone. Once he is wearing my shoes and holding my sword, tell him the truth about his father and send him to meet me."

Aegeus and Aethra then kissed one another and walked to the shore. Boats were waiting for the king there, and he got onto the largest ship and left Troezen forever. Aethra cried softly as she watched his ship sail away and held baby Theseus in her arms tightly. "You will always be the son of a king," she whispered into her little child's ear.

Theseus grew up quickly. It was clear that he would one day be a strong man. As he grew, his mother told him that his father was the god Poseidon, and that he would one day become a great hero because of his good blood. She raised and taught her boy according to the tradition of kings in Troezen and provided him with many famous teachers of arts and war. His knowledge grew quickly, and his skill with the sword could not be beaten by any other young boy in the kingdom.

One day, when Theseus was still a boy, the great hero Hercules came to visit the castle. Hercules was wearing the skin of a lion that he had killed, and when the castle guards saw him they thought that he was a real lion and ran away. Only Theseus was unafraid and stood there with a sword in his hand prepared to fight the animal.

"Well done, young boy," said Hercules laughing. "One day you will become a great hero as strong as I."

Indeed, Theseus grew up to be a very strong and brave man and was unusually smart as well. On Theseus' sixteenth birthday his mother took him to his father's stone.

"Can you lift this stone, Theseus?" she asked.

Theseus lifted the rock easily and found the sword and the shoes that King Aegeus had left there for him.

"Those are gifts left here by your father," his mother said. "He is the leader of a great kingdom over[1] the mountains."

Theseus was surprised to hear this, and said, "But mother, isn't my father the god Poseidon?"

"No, my son," she replied, "Your father is a real man, just like you are. Go to the capital, Athens, and show this sword to the king; he has waited a long time for you to grow up and hopes that you follow him as Athens' next king of Athens."

Theseus was excited to hear this news. Though he had enjoyed thinking that he was the son of a god, he was even happier to know that he had a flesh and blood father whom he could meet and love. He decided to leave for Athens at once.

At that time, most people traveled to Athens by boat because the road to the capital was filled with many dangerous giants. These giants were all very cruel and violent; they enjoyed killing men just for fun. Aethra told her son about all of the terrible giants who waited on the road and asked him not to travel that way, but Theseus told her that he wished to be a great hero and would kill all the giants and make

① **over** = across 越过

the road safe for others.

"I will bring my father his sword covered with the blood of the giants," Theseus told his mother.

Whatever she said, Aethra could not convince him to go to Athens by another way. Theseus packed his things, kissed his mother, and left for Athens.

The Four Giants

Before Theseus had traveled a full day, he met the first giant. This giant was called Periphetes. Periphetes carried a giant club covered with sharp nails and waited in the middle of the road for travelers to pass. Theseus did not slow his walk as he approached the giant; he only reached down for his sword and pulled it from his belt. When he was only a few steps away, the giant raised his weapon and swung it down at Theseus. The young hero jumped quickly to the side and the giant missed. The weapon was so heavy that the giant fell down when he missed hitting Theseus. Theseus saw his opportunity, jumped on the giant's back, and pushed his sword through the back of his huge head. Periphetes never stood up again.

Theseus was proud to have killed his first great enemy and took Periphetes' club with him to remember the fight. After another day of travel Theseus met an old man who warned him of a dangerous giant on the road ahead.

"Do not go any further! There is a giant ahead named Sinis who is very cruel and tricky. He will ask you to help him bend a great pine tree down to the ground. When you have pulled the tree down, he will ask you if you are grasping the tree strongly. When you say 'yes,' he will release his part of the tree and you will be thrown into the air and killed on the rocks below."

Theseus thanked the old man for his warning and continued on his journey. Soon he saw the giant trying to bend a great pine tree down to the ground. When he approached, the giant said, "Young man, you look quite strong. Would you help me pull this tree down to the ground?"

Theseus agreed and the two men pulled the tree down to the ground easily. When the top of the tree was touching the Earth, the giant asked, "Do you have a strong hold of the tree?"

"Not yet!" said Theseus, and released the tree before the giant could let go. The giant flew into the air and came down on a pile of sharp rocks; his head split open on the rocks and he died instantly.

The third giant Theseus met was named Scyron. Scyron lived near a high cliff over the sea and was famous for kicking men off the cliff and sending them to their deaths. However, Theseus had heard of this giant before. When a man passed by, Scyron would demand that they stop to wash his feet. When the man bent down in front of his feet, the giant would kick them back into the sea. The sea was full of large and hungry fish that devoured[①] them. Theseus was sure he could find a way to defeat this giant.

"You may not pass until you wash my feet," yelled the giant when Theseus approached.

"Oh, certainly, great giant!" said Theseus, and the giant sat on a rock by the cliff. Theseus stood in front of him and pretended to reach down to pick up a bucket of water, but, just then, pulled out his sword and cut off the giant's feet. Scyron yelled out in pain and fell to the ground.

"Listen to me now, you cruel giant!" yelled Theseus. "I will cut off your head as well if you do not wash my feet."

① **devour** /dɪˈvaʊə/ *vt.* 狼吞虎咽地吃

The giant was afraid of Theseus now and bent down to wash his feet. Just then Theseus kicked up his leg and the giant fell off the cliff into the sea. The hungry fish found the giant and ate him quickly. Then Theseus continued his journey toward Athens.

Now there was only one more giant to defeat, and his name was Procrustes. Procrustes was the most cruel of all the giants. He invited men into his house to rest, but when they went inside they found that one of his beds was very short and the other was very long. If they lay down in the short bed, Procrustes would take an axe off the wall and cut off their legs so they would fit. If they choose the long bed, Procrustes would tie their arms and legs with rope and pull them until their bodies broke in half. But Theseus had discovered all of this before meeting the giant, and planned to kill him for his cruel ways.

When Theseus was only a few days travel away from Athens, he met Procrustes outside of the giant's house. "Please enter and rest, brave young man!" said the giant.

Theseus entered the giant's house and went into the room with the two beds. Before the giant knew what was happening, Theseus hit him in the head with his club and pushed him down onto the small bed. "It seems that this bed is too short for you," Theseus said while pulling the giant's axe off the wall. He then lifted the axe above his head, brought it down, and cut off Procrustes' legs.

As the giant screamed in pain, Theseus moved his injured body over to the long bed. "This bed is too long for you, giant!" he said. "I will just have to make you longer!" Theseus tied the ropes around Procrustes and pulled him into two pieces. Now all the giants were defeated. Theseus continued on his way to Athens.

Theseus Meets His Father

By the time that Theseus arrived in Athens, his father, King Aegeus, had heard of the young hero who had killed the giants and made the road safe for travelers. The king sent a servant to find the young hero and invite him to the castle. Once found, Theseus accepted the invitation and followed the servant into the castle's main hall[①].

Theseus saw his father from the far end of the hall and was at once filled with great love for the old man. He walked up to the king bravely, pulled out his sword, took off his shoes, and put them down at the king's feet. When the king looked down and saw these things, his heart filled with joy and his eyes filled with tears. To the surprise of all of his guards and servants, he stood up and put his arms around the young man.

With tears running down his face, Aegeus said, "Son, you have finally returned to me. I have waited for sixteen years to see you again, and now I see that you have become a great hero. You will

① **main hall** 正厅

live here with me now and will one day become king yourself."

Indeed, both father and son were very happy that day and lived for many months together. All went well until one morning the young prince woke up to find his father very upset and many of the castle servants crying.

"What's wrong, dear father? Why are you so sad?" he asked.

"Oh, my son, the soldiers from Crete have arrived. They have come to collect seven of our young men and women and take them away."

"Where will they take them?" asked Theseus.

"There is a terrible monster that lives in Crete called the Minotaur—he is a giant man with the head of a bull. Long ago, King Minos of Crete put the Minotaur in a huge maze called the labyrinth. This maze is so large and difficult that no one who enters can ever find their way out. Every nine years King Minos sends men to Athens to collect young men and women to feed to the Minotaur."

"But why must we give the Minotaur our people? Why doesn't King Minos kill his own people instead?" Theseus asked angrily.

Aegeus hung his head sadly. "You see, Theseus, many years ago, we hosted some games to test the athletic ability of young men in the land. Among the athletes who participated in those games was the eldest son of king Minos of Crete, Androgeus."

"Androgeus won many of the events, but the next day he was found murdered. Minos believed that we, the Athenians, had killed his son and demanded that every nine years we send him seven men and seven women, at the age that his son had been, to be fed to the Minotaur. This was to be the payment for his son's murder."

"When I refused to send our young men and women, King Minos started a war with Athens, because his army was stronger, we were defeated. So I had no choice. I had to agree to send our people to the Minotaur."

Theseus learned that this was the third time that the Cretans had come for a collection, and the Athenians were all very unhappy. Every man with a teenaged son or daughter had to draw a number out of a box to determine who would lose his child.

Many people were angry because King Aegeus would not send his own son as a sacrifice[①]. They believed that he was the cause of all their trouble.

Theseus understood the people's anger, so he offered to go to Crete as one of the young people for the Minotaur. All the people of Athens admired the young man for this act. His father tried to change his mind, but the young hero was determined.

"Do not fear, father," Theseus said, "I will kill this monster and Athens will no longer have to send its young men and women to Crete."

"Be very careful, my son, if you die I will not be able to live myself," said Aegeus. "Promise me one thing. When you return from Crete, hang white sails on the ship so that I will know that you are victorious[②]."

"I promise, father," said the young hero.

The ship had black sails while taking the young people to Crete to show the sadness of the task. King Aegeus gave the sailors white sails and ordered them to use the white sails on the return journey, instead of the black ones, if Theseus suc-

① **sacrifice** /ˈsækrɪfaɪs/ *n.* 牺牲品；祭品

② **victorious** /vɪkˈtɔːrɪəs/ *adj.* 胜利的

ceeded in killing the Minotaur.

When the ship arrived in Crete, King Minos ordered that the young men and women stand in a line in front of him. When he saw that one of the young women was very beautiful, he made rude advances① and said that she could live if she became one of his wives. Theseus jumped to defend the girl and said that no Athenian② would marry a man of Crete. This made the king angry, and he stared at the young man with red eyes. He then took a ring off his finger and threw it into the sea.

The king spoke coldly to Theseus, "If you find my ring, I will set this woman free. If not, then I will take her as my bride and do whatever I want with her."

Theseus jumped instantly into the sea and disappeared for many minutes. Just when King Minos believed that he was dead, Theseus' head appeared above the water. He returned to the beach carrying the king's ring in his hand. The king was both angry and surprised to see this. He was afraid that Theseus was some kind of god come to punish him.

---

① **advance** /əd'vɑːns/ *n.* 求爱；追求

② **Athenian** /ə'θiːnɪən/ *n.* 雅典人

Because of his fear, he decided to keep his promise[①] and let the girl go. He then ordered his soldiers to bring the rest of the young people, including Theseus, to the palace.

① **keep one's promise** 信守诺言

Theseus and the Minotaur

King Minos sat in his high chair and watched the young Athenians enter his great hall. "You all know that you will never leave the labyrinth alive," said Minos. "The Minotaur will find you and kill you one by one."

"But what if we kill the Minotaur first, King Minos?" said Theseus.

Minos laughed loudly. "Kill the Minotaur?" he said. "Why, if you kill the Minotaur, I promise to let all of you go."

"I will kill him," said Theseus. "Just let me take my sword into the labyrinth[①], and I will face the monster."

"Oh, so the lucky swimmer is now a hero too!" said Minos. He was still laughing.

"I am Theseus, son of King Aegeus. If I kill your monster, will you promise to let us return to Athens?"

"All right, tomorrow morning you may try to

① **labyrinth** /ˈlæbərɪnθ/ *n.* 迷宫

kill my monster. If you escape the labyrinth, all of you may leave."

Ariadne[①], King Minos' daughter, was standing next to her father as the men spoke. She thought Theseus was very handsome and admired his courage so much that she fell in love with him instantly. She secretly decided to help the young hero.

During the night, Ariadne quietly went into the prisoners' room and awoke Theseus. She explained to Theseus that the Minotaur was not his only danger.

"Who are you?" Theseus said and admired her beauty.

"I am Ariadne, the daughter of the king, and I am here to help you. Listen to me. You will enter the labyrinth easily, and I believe that you are a great hero and will kill the Minotaur. But even if you do that, you will never find your way out of the maze! You see, even the Minotaur is a prisoner there. But I know how you can escape the labyrinth. If I tell you how to get out of the labyrinth, will you promise to marry me and take me with you to Athens?"

Theseus promised the princess that he would

① **Ariadne**【希神】阿里阿德涅，迈诺斯和帕西法尔的女儿，曾给忒修斯一个线团，帮助他走出弥诺陶洛斯的迷宫。

do so, and then Ariadne gave him a ball of thin string and explained to him what to do.

The next morning when Theseus entered the labyrinth, he tied one end of the string to a rock near the door. As he walked deeper into the maze, he let the string out slowly. Theseus walked deeper and deeper into the maze, always moving towards the center where the Minotaur lived. The bones of many people and animals lay on the ground. Many of the walls were covered with dry blood.

Eventually Theseus heard the sound of heavy breathing and the loud footsteps of a large animal. He stopped walking and waited for the Minotaur to appear around the corner. As soon as the monster saw Theseus, it put its head down and ran at Theseus with its horns. Theseus reached out his strong arms and grabbed the horns with his powerful hands. The Minotaur turned its head quickly back and forth[①] trying to get Theseus off, but it could not. Then Theseus used all his strength and turned the Minotaur's neck until it almost broke. The Minotaur fell and, before it could get back up again,

① **back and forth** 来回地，往返地

Theseus pushed his sword into its mouth and all the way through its head. He then followed the string back to the entrance to the labyrinth.

When Theseus came out of the labyrinth with a bloody sword in his hands, the other Athenians began crying tears of joy. By killing the Minotaur, Theseus had not only saved his own life, but theirs as well. King Minos was very angry to see Theseus come out of the labyrinth alive. However, because of his amazing deed, the king was now certain that Theseus was protected by the gods. He let the Athenians go free, and thus Athens' debt to Crete was ended.

The next day, Theseus kept his promise to Ariadne and took her with him. When King Minos learned that his daughter had left with Theseus, he sent his ships to capture[①] the Athenians. But Theseus had left very early, and his ship was too far ahead. After following for just a day, Minos' ships gave up and returned to Crete.

Everyone was so happy returning to Athens that they had a great party and drank all the wine

① **capture** /'kæptʃə/ *vt.* 俘虏，捕获

on the ship. The next day they stopped on the island of Naxos[①] and went in search of[②] fresh water. While on the island, Ariadne walked around picking flowers to give to Theseus. She soon fell asleep on the beach in the warm sun. When Theseus saw her sleeping there, a strange thing happened. His heart turned cold to her, and he ordered his people to return to the ship and leave the island without her. Ariadne awoke just in time to see the ship disappear from sight. Her heart broke, and she cried until night fell.

When the gods heard Ariadne cry, they became angry and decided to punish Theseus for his selfishness. They made all the people on the ship forget to hang the white sails. As they approached Athens, the black sails still hung high.

Since Theseus had left, his father had spent every day sitting on a high cliff over the sea—watching the water and waiting for the ship's return. When he saw the black sails hung on the ship, his heart broke just as Ariadne's. He had prayed all his life that his son would rule the

① **Naxos** 纳克索斯岛，爱琴海（the Aegean Sea）东南部的一个岛屿。

② **in search of** 寻找

kingdom after he died, and now he did not have anyone to rule the kingdom after he died. He stood up and walked over to the edge of the cliff, looked once more at the black sails on the ship, and let himself fall into the sea far below.

When Theseus finally arrived in Athens, he expected a large party to be going on in celebration of the safe return of the young men and women. Instead all the people had sad faces, and Theseus was greeted only by the dead body of his father, lying on the beach where the waves had pushed it.

Bellerophon and the Winged Horse Pegasus

Long ago there lived a great king named Sisyphus who ruled one of Greece's many kingdoms. He had a daughter who was beautiful and kindhearted and loved by all the men in the land. This beautiful girl loved the sea and spent a lot of time walking on the beach and watching the waves. One day she returned to the castle wet with sea water. When Sisyphus asked why she was wet, she refused to reply.

Exactly nine months after that day, she gave birth to a son. When Sisyphus demanded that she tell him who the father was, she again refused to answer. She named her son Bellerophon and raised him with all the love a mother could give. Later she had a second son and called him Deliades.

Bellerophon grew up into a strong and brave young man. People all over the land admired his great skill in fighting, and all women said he was as handsome as he was strong. Everyone wondered who his father was, for certainly his father must be a great hero. Many people said that his father was actually the god of the sea, Poseidon. No one could say for certain that Bellerophon was the son of a god, but many people believed that he was. Bellerophon, himself, believed that he was a god's son.

One day while they were out hunting together, Bellerophon accidentally killed his brother Deliades with an arrow. This angered Sisyphus greatly, and he ordered his men to find Bellerophon and punish him. Bellerophon had not intended to kill his brother and wanted to avoid the punishment, so he left his homeland and escaped to the land of Tiryns. Once in Tiryns, Bellerophon went to meet the king and offer him his strength and services.

Tiryns was ruled by a king named Proteus and his wife, Anteia. The people of Tiryns were always very kind to their guests and had many laws saying that guests should be treated like a member of your own family. Due to this, Proteus invited Bellerophon to stay in the castle for as long as he wanted.

While living in the castle, Queen Anteia grew to like Bellerophon and desired him for his youth and beauty. One night she went to his room and asked him to sleep with her. However, Bellerophon refused and demanded that she leave his room at once. The queen felt so angry and embarrassed by Bellerophon's actions that she decided to take revenge on[①] him. With this in mind, she told her husband that Bellerophon had tried to rape her.

Hearing this made Proteus red with anger, but he dared not kill Bellerophon, for the laws of the land said that one could not hurt their own guest. So instead of killing Bellerophon himself Proteus decided to have someone else do it for him. He gave Bellerophon a closed letter and asked him to bring it to Anteia's father, King Iobates. Bellerophon accepted the task happily, for he was anxious to repay all of Proteus' kindness. Inside the letter, Proteus wrote:

The man carrying this letter tried to rape your daughter Anteia. I have sent him to you for punishment. King Proteus.

However Proteus's plan for Bellerophon's death failed. Iobates also had to follow the laws of the land and could not harm a guest. Instead, he

① **take revenge on** 向……报复

thought of a plan to trick the young man into going to his death himself.

In Iobates' kingdom lived a terrible monster called the Chimaera. The monster had the body of a lion and three different heads. In addition to the normal lion head, there was also a large snake head and the head of a goat. Strangely enough, the goat's head was the most dangerous of the three, because that head could breathe out fire.

Killing the Chimaera was a terrible and dangerous task, and Iobates felt sure that Bellerophon would be killed if he fought the monster. One day, the old king told Bellerophon about the Chimaera and told him about how it was killing his people and destroying the countryside. "If some brave man could kill this monster he would be a hero in the hearts of all my people!" said the king, looking at Bellerophon.

When Bellerophon heard the king's words, he jumped up and said that he himself would kill the Chimaera and end the people's fear. Bellerophon knew that this task was almost impossible, but he felt that king Iobates had been a very good host to him and wanted to repay his kindness. Still, Bellerophon did not have any idea how he could kill the Chimaera. Before facing the monster, he decided to find Polyeides, a man of great wisdom and learning who lived in Iobates' kingdom. Polyeides had once been a great hero himself, but he had since grown old and moved to a small house far away from other people.

Polyeides told Bellerophon that the only way for one man to defeat the Chimaera was if he could fly. "If you attacked the Chimaera from above," Polyeides explained, "you would have a great advantage over① the monster."

Bellerophon was confused and asked, "But how can I fly in the sky? I am not a bird."

"You must go and capture the great and beautiful Pegasus, the white-winged horse that lives in the magic forest to the east," said Polyeides. "First pray to the gods and ask for their help in this difficult task. Then search for Pegasus."

Following Polyeides's instructions, Bellerophon spent the entire night praying to the gods and ask-

① **have a great advantage over** 比……有很大的优势

ing for their help. Bellerophon did not fall asleep until the sun came up over the mountains. When Bellerophon awoke, he found a golden horse bridle[①] on the ground beside him. The bridle had been left there by the goddess Athena. Bellerophon was happy, for he knew that the gods supported him in his task.

After searching the magic forest for several days, Bellerophon finally found Pegasus drinking water from a river. Holding the golden bridle in one hand, Bellerophon carefully approached the amazing animal. The horse noticed him coming closer and turned his head towards Bellerophon's and looked in his eyes. For a moment, Bellerophon feared that Pegasus would fly away. However, to his surprise, the horse again put his head down to the water and continued to drink.

Slowly, Bellerophon reached out to touch Pegasus and put the golden bridle on his head. Pegasus did not fight or argue and waited calmly as Bellerophon climbed onto his back. An instant later, Pegasus had jumped into the air and flew quickly

① **bridle** /ˈbraɪdl/ *n.* 马笼头

upward. Soon Bellerophon found himself high among the clouds. All day, Bellerophon flew high in the sky looking down at the land below. In his heart, Bellerophon felt like a god flying in the heavens. It was a wonderful feeling! He was sure that his father must have been a god, or else Pegasus would not have let him ride her.

The next day, Bellerophon collected together some weapons. He prepared a sword, bow, arrows, and a thick coat and rode Pegasus to find the Chimaera. Due to Pegasus' great speed, he quickly found the monster. Pegasus flew down at the monster, and Bellerophon swung at it with his sword. The Chimaera's goat head breathed fire at Bellerophon, but Pegasus was too fast and escaped the monster's attack. Then Bellerophon pulled out an arrow and prepared his bow. His very first shot went through the neck that all three of the Chimaera's heads shared. The monster tried to let out a sound of pain, but only blood came out of its three terrible mouths.

With the monster dead and his task complete, Bellerophon returned to Iobates' castle to give him

the news. He expected Iobates would thank him for his heroic deed, but, strangely, the king looked angry and gave Bellerophon another dangerous task. Bellerophon completed this task successfully as well and was given another. Each time, Bellerophon succeeded, he received yet another dangerous mission. Soon Iobates realized that Bellerophon was not going to be killed on these dangerous missions.

So, Iobates decided to ignore the law and kill Bellerophon directly. He sent ten of his bravest and most skilled soldiers to kill Bellerophon. But to Iobates' surprise, Bellerophon killed them all. Iobates was amazed by Bellerophon's skill and began to think that Bellerophon was protected by the gods. At this same time, Bellerophon finally realized that Iobates had wanted him to fail in his dangerous tasks. And now, the king had sent men to kill him. But why? Bellerophon had no idea.

Bellerophon was a brave man and decided to talk with Iobates directly. When he spoke with the Iobates, the king showed him the letter from King Proteus. Bellerophon was shocked and explained the true situation with Anteia. When the king heard

Bellerophon's story, he believed him and was deeply sorry for trying to kill him. To show his thanks for all the great deeds that Bellerophon had done for his kingdom, King Iobates offered Bellerophon his youngest daughter, Philonoe, in marriage. Bellerophon accepted and became the prince of the kingdom and enjoyed great wealth and comfort.

However, after a few years of marriage, Bellerophon became bored of the life of a prince. He felt that his heroic deeds had proven that he was certainly the son of a god. His pride began to grow, until finally he became convinced being a prince was not a great enough honor for him. He wanted to become a god, not remain a common man. He was determined to join the gods in heaven, even if he had to use force!

Bellerophon collected his weapons and climbed onto Pegasus once more. With his sword in hand, he ordered Pegasus up into the sky, toward the top of Mt①. Olympus where all the gods lived. Zeus, the king of the gods, watched the foolish man as he flew toward heaven and was angry that a common man

① **Mt. = mountain** /'maʊntən/ *n.* 山峰

would dare attack the gods. He was about to throw lightning at Bellerophon to kill him, but he did not want to hurt Pegasus, who was loved by the gods. Instead, he sent a bee to sting[①] Pegasus under his tail. When Pegasus felt the sting, jumped up suddenly and threw Bellerophon off his back.

Bellerophon fell all the way back down to Earth. The great fall did not kill him, but he was terribly injured. The gods had allowed Bellerophon to survive[②] his fall. His body was broken in many places and he could no longer use his arms and legs well. His head was hit so hard that he was no longer able to see or speak. With his body and heart broken, the once great hero wandered the earth alone, blind, unhappy, and unknown to any man. He had been loved by the gods, but his foolishness and pride had made them angry. The rest of his sad life was his punishment. They had decided that a quick death was not punishment enough for him, and wanted him to suffer for many years.

No one knows when and where Bellerophon died. Nor does anyone really know whether Bel-

① **sting** /stɪŋ/ *vt.*（指植物或昆虫）叮，蜇

② **survive** /səˈvaɪv/ *vt.* 幸免于难

lerophon was really the son of Poseidon or just a common man. Regardless of[①] whom his father was, Bellerophon's fortune was decided when he attacked Mt. Olympus.

Pegasus' fortune was quite different, however. After Pegasus threw Bellerophon off his back, she was welcomed into Mt. Olympus. She lived forever among the gods and goddess and wandered freely in Heaven and on Earth.

① **regardless of** 不管，不顾